ויקבץ נדחי עמו ישראל, *Children from all over the world are returning to Torah at the Hebrew Academy of West Queens*

והשיב לב אבות על בנים, *And he shall return the hearts of the fathers through the sons.*

Hebrew Academy of West Queens

The Hebrew Academy of West Queens was established to perpetuate the traditional ideals of our heritage, to teach Torah to our children, so that they will have both the inspiration and understanding to live as observant Jews. From its inception, the Yeshiva has been in the forefront of the "kiruv" movement, igniting the flame of Yiddishkeit in thousands of American public school and immigrant children who would have been lost to assimilation.

Over the past twenty-eight years, the school has provided thousands of these children with a Torah true education. Its graduates have become outstanding students in many of the well-known Yeshiva institutions. The two-hundred and eighty students currently enrolled in the Yeshiva in Jackson Heights come from neighborhoods throughout the metropolitan area.

What distinguishes the Hebrew Academy of West Queens from Yeshivas that cater exclusively to immigrant children? At the Hebrew Academy immigrant children are placed in a setting where they interact with and learn from veteran Yeshiva students. Immigrant students who have already become Torah oriented have a very positive effect on new arrivals. The Yeshiva and its dedicated staff impart our heritage in an environment where both advanced and beginning students from all backgrounds and cultures can flourish.

34-25 82nd Street / Jackson Heights N.Y. 11372 / (718) 899-9193

Harav Henoch Liebowitz, Shlita, Rosh HaYeshiva of Rabbinical Seminary of America in Forest Hills, comes to distribute the first Gemara and render encouraging words to our 5th and 6th grade boys.

In Memory of

Hyman Fein

ר' חיים ב"ר ראובן ע"ה

Our very dear friend and officer of
the Yeshiva for over twenty years
whose enthusiasm, loyal devotion
and benevolent generosity have
forged an eternal bond with our Yeshiva.

His dedication and deep-rooted concern
remain an inspiration to all who were
privileged to work with him.

Hebrew Academy of West Queens

Mr. Bernard Zyniewski, *President*
Mr. Ludwig Katz, *Vice President*
Mrs. Iris Fein, *Secretary*
Rabbi Moshe Stahler, *Dean*
Rabbi David Feldstein, *Administrator*

In Memory of

Morris and Anna Hulkower

Louis and Rose Zyniewski

Lee Zyniewski

Libby Alperowitz

Helen Goodman

In Memory of

Benjamin Solkoff

and

Paul Ledet

from

Rose Solkoff

Dora Ledet

Irving and Arlene Solkoff

Leslie Ledet

David and Elycia

Joseph and Judy Marmo

Daniel and Bonnie

In Memory of
our beloved husband,
father, grandfather, brother,
brother-in-law and uncle

Mr. Aaron Levinson

ר׳ אהרן ב״ר יהודה ע״ה

Mrs. Sylvia Levinson
Annette and Joel Levinson and Family
Nechama and William Liss-Levinson and Family
Vera and Jesse Weisberger and Family
Shirley and Seymour Levinson and Family
Myra and Sam Lerner and Family
Nancy and Julian Lerner and Family
Edith Lerner

In honor of

our dear cousins

Rabbi Moshe and Miriam Stahler

Whose selfless devotion

to the Yeshiva knows no bounds.

Their sincere dedication

to instilling a love for Torah and Yiddishkeit

to the students of the

Hebrew Academy of West Queens

is evident to all those

who are fortunate to know them.

May השי״ת grant them the strength

to continue in their holy endeavor

and be זוכה to health, happiness and נחת.

**Esti and Ushi Stahler
and Family**

לזכר נשמות

ר' יצחק ב"ר אברהם יעקב

מאלה בת ר' מרדכי יוסף

מישל בת ר' יצחק

גיטל בת ר' יצחק

אברהם יעקב ב"ר יצחק

למשפחת ראזענבוש

ר' זאב ב"ר חיים צבי

יוטא בת ר' חיים יוסף

יעקב יצחק ב"ר זאב

חנה ליבא בת ר' זאב

ישראל מרדכי ב"ר זאב

משה יהודה ב"ר זאב

למשפחת פעלדשטיין

Mr. and Mrs. Abraham Feldstein and Family

In loving memory
of our dear husband, father and grandfather

Paul Mittel

ר' יששכר ב"ר דניאל הלוי ע"ה

שנלב"ע בערב שבת נחמו נחמו עמי

ט"ו באב תשנ"ב

A man who dedicated his life
to imparting his love for Torah and devotion
to the Hebrew Academy of West Queens
to his children and grandchildren.

May his memory be an inspiration
and may our commitment to Yiddishkeit
become his legacy.

Mrs. Ruth Mittel
Mr. & Mrs. Daniel Mittel
Mr. & Mrs. Harold Mittel
Mr. & Mrs. Kenny Mittel
Rabbi & Mrs. Abe Jakubowicz
Mr. & Mrs. Mark Mittel
and Families

לזכר נשמות

אבא מורי

אברהם אבא בן אהרן אליעזר

סקאלער ע״ה

אמא מורתי

האשה חיה בת דוד הכהן

סקאלער ע״ה

In memory of

Max Hecht

מרדכי בן ר׳ שמואל העבט ע״ה

לזכר נשמות

ר׳ יוסף בן ר׳ יעקב ע״ה
מרת פייגא בת ר׳ יעקב ע״ה
ר׳ חיים יהושע בן ר׳ דוד ע״ה
מרת שרה פייגא בת ר׳ חיים יהושע ע״ה
ר׳ משה אהרן בן ר׳ דוד הלוי ע״ה

In loving memory of

Joseph and Fanny Leitner

Hyman Stahler

Sandra Fay Stahler

Morris Zharnest

Their lifelong dedication to Torah education
continues to be an inspiration to us
their children and grandchildren

Rabbi and Mrs. Moshe Stahler

Yaakov and Yosefa

Rabbi and Mrs. David Zharnest

Shira Chaya, Aharon Yehoshua
and Yitzchok Yosef

לזכר נשמות

חיה בת ר׳ אליעזר הלוי סראלאוויטש

ר׳ נפתלי בן ר׳ רפאל פרווידינבערגער

אסתר בת ר׳ יחיאל מיכל ווינקלער

May their exemplary lives of devotion to Torah and chesed be an inspiration to their children, grandchildren and great grandchildren

**Mr. and Mrs. Allen Szrolovits
and Family**

"תורת חיים ואהבת חסד וצדקה"

In loving memory of
our dear parents

Nechemiah and Rivka Korn

לז"נ

ר' נחמי' ב"ר שלום הלוי ז"ל

נפטר ז' טבת, תשמ"ה

לז"נ

מרת רבקה בת ר' יהושע ז"ל

נפטרה י"ז תשרי, תשמ"ה

whose lives were steeped in Torah and Yiras Shomayim,
dedicating themselves to the establishment
and perpetuation of Torah institutions
and who taught us the true meaning
of Tzedokoh and G'milus Chassodim

With deep appreciation for this legacy they left behind

Henny and Yaakov Krasner
Chaim Korn
Fannie and Abe Bornstein
Ruthie and Yossi Dresdner

In grateful appreciation to

the trustees and supporters of

The Susan Chesner Einbinder Memorial Fund

whose continued support

has enabled many of our students

to enrich their lives with

the study of Torah.

May Hashem grant them

continued success in

all of their endeavors.

מסורה

ArtScroll Mesorah Series®

Rabbi Nosson Scherman / Rabbi Meir Zlotowitz
General Editors

A MACHZOR COMPANION

The themes of the High Holy Days Machzor

by
Rabbi Moshe Eisemann

Published by
Mesorah Publications, ltd

FIRST EDITION
First Impression . . . August 1993

Published and Distributed by
MESORAH PUBLICATIONS, Ltd.
Brooklyn, New York 11232

Distributed in Israel by
MESORAH MAFITZIM / J. GROSSMAN
Rechov Harav Uziel 117
Jerusalem, Israel

Distributed in Australia & New Zealand by
GOLD'S BOOK & GIFT CO.
36 William Street
Balaclava 3183, Vic., Australia

Distributed in Europe by
J. LEHMANN HEBREW BOOKSELLERS
20 Cambridge Terrace
Gateshead, Tyne and Wear
England NE8 1RP

Distributed in South Africa by
KOLLEL BOOKSHOP
22 Muller Street
Yeoville 2198
Johannesburg, South Africa

THE ARTSCROLL MESORAH SERIES®
A MACHZOR COMPANION

© *Copyright 1993, by* MESORAH PUBLICATIONS, Ltd.
4401 Second Avenue / Brooklyn, N.Y. 11232 / (718) 921-9000

ALL RIGHTS RESERVED.

No part of this book may be reproduced
in any form *without* **written** *permission from the copyright holder,*
except by a reviewer who wishes to quote brief passages in connection with a review
written for inclusion in magazines or newspapers.

THE RIGHTS OF THE COPYRIGHT HOLDER WILL BE STRICTLY ENFORCED.

ISBN
0-89906-425-6 (hard cover)
0-89906-426-4 (paperback)

Typography by Compuscribe at ArtScroll Studios, Ltd.

Printed in the United States of America by Noble Book Press
Bound by Sefercraft, Quality Bookbinders, Ltd. Brooklyn, N.Y.

⋐ Table of Contents

Rosh Hashanah

Today Eternity Is Conceived	10
Today He Places All the Creatures of the World Before the Bar of Justice	16
Perhaps He Will Look Upon Us As Children	23
Perhaps He Will Look Upon Us As Servants	30
Remember Us For Life . . .	36
Who is Like You Merciful Father . . .	43
Inscribe All Those With Whom You Have Forged Your Covenant for a Good Life	50
In the Book of Life, Blessing and Peace and Good Livelihood . . .	56
Now This Being So, O Hashem Our God Instill All Those Whom You Made With Your Awe . . .	60
Our God and the God of Our Forefathers, Reign Over the Entire Universe in Your Glory . . .	72
You Remember Actions Taken From the Beginning of Time	87
. . . And Accompanied by a Shofar Blast Did You Appear to Them . . .	93

Yom Kippur

The Entire Family of Israel Shall Be Forgiven	107
For We Are Not Brazen Faced . . .	127
O Vigorously Strong . . .	136
Hail His Illustrious Kingship To All Eternity	143
What Is Our Value? What Is the Value of Our Lives?	152
The Shofar and the Nail	162

Rosh Hashanah
ראש השנה

הַיּוֹם הֲרַת עוֹלָם, הַיּוֹם יַעֲמִיד בַּמִּשְׁפָּט,
כָּל יְצוּרֵי עוֹלָמִים,
אִם כְּבָנִים, אִם כַּעֲבָדִים.
אִם כְּבָנִים, רַחֲמֵנוּ כְּרַחֵם אָב עַל בָּנִים;
וְאִם כַּעֲבָדִים עֵינֵינוּ לְךָ תְלֻיוֹת,
עַד שֶׁתְּחָנֵּנוּ וְתוֹצִיא כָאוֹר מִשְׁפָּטֵנוּ,
אָיוֹם קָדוֹשׁ.

Today is the birth[day] of the world.
Today all creatures of the world stand in judgment —
whether as children [of God] or as servants.
If as children, be merciful with us
as the mercy of a father for children.
If as servants, our eyes look toward and depend upon You,
until You be gracious to us and release our verdict
clear and pure as light,
O Awesome and Holy One.

הַיּוֹם הֲרַת עוֹלָם ❧
Today Eternity Is Conceived

The shofar has sounded. The moment has come. We stand before God. We, weighed down with our puniness and our vulnerability, our pretenses and our shames, our hopes and our despairs, our prayers and our secrets, our bravado and our terrors, have become the primary focus of God's attention. Naked and alone — as Adam long ago in Eden — we must face the consequences of what we have chosen to make of our lives.

Our past is about to forge our future.

In this dreadful moment. For each of us — eternity is conceived.[1]

And how?

Because: *Today He places all creatures of the world before the bar of justice* (... יַעֲמִיד בַּמִּשְׁפָּט).

---

1. In the ArtScroll *machzor*, the phrase, הַיּוֹם הֲרַת עוֹלָם is rendered, *Today is the birth[day] of the world*. The commentators do, indeed, offer this meaning although it is difficult to find a clear instance in which the root, הרה has the connotation, *to give birth* rather than, *to conceive*. See note in *machzor* on p.509.

In this interpretation the flow from the thought, *Today is the birth[day] of the world* to, *Today all creatures of the world stand in judgment*, is not entirely clear. Certainly the idea that the day of creation may be an ideal day for God to sit in judgment over us is not a difficult one and, in the course of these essays, we will come back to it. Nevertheless the connection is not so obvious that the author should not have found it necessary to provide some kind of bridge between the two ideas. In the interpretation which we offer, the thought-flow is simple. Today eternity is conceived *because* today He places all the creatures of the world before the bar of justice.

The phrase, הֲרַת עוֹלָם occurs in *Jeremiah* 20:17 in a passage in which the prophet curses the day upon which he was born. The verse reads as follows: *[Woe] that He did not kill me while I was yet in the womb, so that my mother might have been my grave, and her womb — a conception to eternity* [הֲרַת עוֹלָם

What precisely is the concept which underlies the Torah idea of מִשְׁפָּט, *judgment*?

It is no accident that both the word, מִשְׁפָּט and its synonym חֹק carry the connotation, *custom* or *usage* in addition to their base meaning of *judgment*.[2] Thus, *Ramban* to *Exodus* 15:28: ... For custom [מִנְהָג] is expressed by the word חֹק as in הַטְרִיפֵנִי לֶחֶם חֻקִּי (*Proverbs* 30:8) ... and is also called מִשְׁפָּט in as much as it describes a well-balanced situation [בהיותו משוער כהוגן]. Thus, כֹּה עָשָׂה דָוִד וְכֹה מִשְׁפָּטוֹ כָּל הַיָּמִים (*I Samuel* 27:11).

Custom and *usage* are habits which are assumed because they fit smoothly into a given situation and fill the needs which inhere in it. Thus, for example, in the text which *Ramban* is explaining in the comments which we quoted above, ... שָׁם שָׂם לוֹ חֹק וּמִשְׁפָּט, describes, as he understands it, the rules which Moses imposed upon the people in order to make their travels through the awesome desert as efficient and bearable as possible.

Accordingly, we conclude that the Torah views *mishpat* as an *ordering*, a re-establishing of context and association. Two

---

וְרָחְמָה]. The sense is that life is temporary but death, eternal. Had Jeremiah died in the womb then the earlier conception would have been one to eternity [death] whereas now that he was born it resulted in a temporary state [life].

Thus, in its original usage, the phrase carries the translation which we have used: *eternity is conceived*. It is my contention that even if we were to accept that the *paytan* borrowed the phrase for the *machzor* and in the new context invested it with new meaning, it still, for the perceptive reader, subliminally recalls its earlier message. Thus, our contemplation of the phrase as we have rendered it remains germane and appropriate even if we accept the alternative translation as authoritative.

2. We assume that the two phrases in כִּי חֹק לְיִשְׂרָאֵל הוּא מִשְׁפָּט לֵאלֹהֵי יַעֲקֹב (*Psalms* 81:5) are to be understood as a simple parallelism and that, accordingly חֹק is a synonym of מִשְׁפָּט. This accords with *Ibn Ezra* there, although *Rashi* and *Metzudos* understand the phrase differently. We make this assumption in the context of our thoughts concerning the *machzor* because that seems to be how the *paytan* uses the word in phrases like, חֹק זִכָּרוֹן (*Zichronos*, *Musaf*).

Radak, *Sefer HaShorashim* also has the word connote, *judgment* but reaches that conclusion from a different perspective. The root, חקק, in his view, means, *to write* and the association with judgment, where there is usually someone recording the proceedings, derives from this meaning.

litigants argue about ownership or obligation. An asymmetry has intruded upon the orderly societal structure which earlier had bound the two into a peaceful and intermeshing relationship. It is the function of the judge to sort out the claims, to create harmony in place of dissonance, and to position the two, in relation to each other and to society, where positive and fruitful engagement would have them.

The proposition that the essence of justice is the restoration of a harmony that had been compromised by quarrel, can be extended to the *mishpat* of the sinner as he stands before God to give an accounting for his actions. That too, surprisingly enough, can be viewed as litigation — this time between God and man.

> ... My friend had a vineyard. [It lay] in a rich and fertile cove.
>
> He fenced it; smoothed it; planted it with choice vines; provided it with a watchman's tower and even sunk a vat at its center. He anticipated [a harvest of] luscious grapes.
>
> Instead, it produced stinking rot.
>
> And now ... decide, if you will [שָׁפְטוּ נָא], between me and my vineyard.
>
> What more than what I have already done is there to do for my vineyard? Why should it have produced stinking rot in place of the grapes for which I had hoped?
>
> Now I will let you know what I will do to my vineyard: [I] will have its protective hedge removed so that it will turn into grazing land; [I] will have its wall breached so that it becomes trampled.
>
> I will lay it desolate; it shall be neither pruned nor hoed so that thorns and thistle choke it. I shall command the clouds not to release rain upon it.
>
> For the House of Israel is the vineyard of HASHEM *Tzevaos*, and Judah's men are the saplings in which

He took delight. He had hoped for justice, and see, a leprous blotch! For charity, and see, a wailing! (*Isaiah 5:1-7*).

God has, the right to demand that we pattern our behavior in accordance with that unstinting love which we so liberally receive at His hands. We are, quite literally, obliged to act with justice and charity because we are the direct beneficiaries of His passion for truth, His boundless goodness. When our lives reek of the putrid ugliness of sin, we have wronged not only ourselves but Him. We have befouled a relationship which He treasures, have sown discord where there should be only love, have cast the orderly symmetry that sets rights honestly earned against obligations conscientiously rendered, into disarray. He has the moral right to summon us to the bar of justice. He may demand not only restitution but retribution. Both are needed if *mishpat* is to take its course, if an ambience of finely balanced relationships is to be reestablished.

But sin throws much more than our correct standing before God into disarray. Each of us are both children and parents, products of a past that reaches to the dawn of history, progenitors of a future that reverberates to our actions and failings to the end of time. We function within a complex matrix of interlocking relationships which guarantees that, in subtle ways indiscernible to the human eye but clear to all-seeing God, we leave nothing and nobody untouched by either our strengths or our frailties.

Thus, the introduction to *Zichronos*:

> You remember ... all the creatures fashioned *since earliest times* ... all hidden things are revealed and the multitude of mysteries *since the beginning of Creation* for there is no forgetfulness before Your throne ... Everything is revealed and known before You ... Who keeps watch and sees *to the very end of all generations* ...

היום הרת עולם — *Eternity Conceived*

We quote from *Rinas Chaim*, the analysis of the Rosh Hashanah and Yom Kippur prayers by the late *mashgiach* of Ponievez, R' Chaim Friedlander.

> ... Judgment is executed from a vantage point which considers all that is past, the present, and that which still lies in the future. אַתָּה זוֹכֵר מַעֲשֵׂה עוֹלָם is the *past*; אַתָּה זוֹכֵר אֶת כָּל הַמִּפְעָל is the *present*; הַכֹּל גָּלוּי וְיָדוּעַ is the *future*.
>
> Why?
>
> Because it is Israel's historic function to bring creation to perfection and to nudge it towards ultimate fulfillment by means of their good deeds. This function is spread among all Jews up to the time of *Mashiach*. Each individual has his specific part to play. This is much like a single link in a chain of the generations. Now when a single link does not perform as it should, then there is a dislocation in the functioning of all the generations.
>
> Therefore each individual is considered within the context which must take past, present and future into consideration. This because his actions must be judged beneficial or harmful within the structure of sanctity which is to be built by the combined labor of all the generations ...

Every second of this awesome day is laden with frightening and somber portent. In each of us a world is concealed. Of all these worlds the World is made. We carry its fate in our hearts and hands. Empowered to be giants we know ourselves to be dwarfs. Across the centuries, carried in the roars and whisperings of nature and history, we hear the one dreadful question thrusting and jabbing through our sorry defenses, piercing cruelly through the facade of equanimity with which, at other times, we make life possible: אַיֶּכָּה! What has become of you?

What answer can we give? How can we make our way back to an Eden which we allowed to slip through our hands?

Why is it just *today* that He places all the creatures of the world before the bar of justice?

What is this Rosh Hashanah before which we tremble so?

הַיוֹם יַעֲמִיד בַּמִשְׁפָּט כָּל יְצוּרֵי עוֹלָמִים ◆§
Today He Places All the Creatures of the World Before the Bar of Justice

Why the stress on *today*? Clearly the fact that both the previous phrase, [הַיוֹם הֲרַת עוֹלָם], and our's give the word הַיוֹם the pride of first position, indicates that there is something very special about this particular day.

Rosh Hashanah, from the very first moment that we meet up against it seems shrouded in mystery. *Now in the seventh month, on the first day of the month there shall occur for you a sacred convocation. It shall be for you a day of rememberance generated by a [shofar] blast. You shall perform no manner of work* (*Leviticus* 23:23). We are given no hint at all to help us understand why this day among all others was chosen for singularity. What is to be *remembered*? Why by means of a [shofar] blast? And why, above all, on this particular day?

Rosh Hashanah is the only one of the *Yamim Tovim* which the Torah treats with such reticence. The time and content assigned to Pesach are self explanatory. Shavuos, while only its agricultural aspect is mentioned — never that at its heart is the celebration of *Mattan Torah* (see below for *Maharal's* thought on this subject) — is tied to Pesach through the counting of the *Sefirah*, and thus a context is provided. There is no apparent logic to the date assigned to Succos, but the idea of a *Yom Tov* devoted to the contemplation of our desert experiences is natural. The Torah identifies Yom Kippur as a day upon which God grants atonement for our sins and a simple computation using the dates given for God's appearance on Sinai and the giving of the *Luchos* provides an understanding for the special significance of the tenth of Tishrei.

But there is absolutely nothing in the Torah which would explain why any importance attaches to the *first day of the seventh month*, nor why or for what purpose the shofar is to be sounded on that day, nor again, what *memory* is meant to be awakened.

The Oral Law, of course, fleshes out the written account. The date designated by the Torah is that of the Friday of creation, the day that man first appeared upon the earth. The [shofar] blast is to usher in the moment of God's awesome judgment — the accounting which he demands, upon this anniversary, of the use to which we have put this wonderful world which He so unstintingly gave us. [1]

But of all this there is no hint at all in the written Torah.

It is as though the Torah as it is written [though of course we know the reason from *Torah Shebe'al Peh*], wishes us to embark upon a journey of discovery, a searching for the essence and meaning of this day — and within that search, and as part of it, to burrow onwards and inwards into our own essence, until we have laid bare the meaning and implications of our own lives.

Where is our search to lead us? Against which standards are we to measure ourselves? Why, if הַיוֹם הֲרַת עוֹלָם means, *Today is the birth[day] of the world* (see previous essay), does the *paytan* wish to transport us back to Eden?

❈ ❈ ❈

The recitation of *Malchios*, *Zichronos* and *Shoforos* occupies a central position in our Rosh Hashanah prayers. We shall come back to each of these concepts individually in later essays. For now we wish to address an unexpected peculiarity in the matter of *Malchios*.

---

1. The association between the concept, זִכָּרוֹן and *judgment* is traced by Ramban (*Drashah LeRosh Hashanah*) to Ezekiel 18:22 and 24; 21:28 and 29; Psalms 25:7; Nehemiah 5:19. (But see *Maharal* below who disagrees with this interpretation of זִכָּרוֹן.)

We go to *Rosh Hashanah* 32a where the Gemara attempts to find a Scriptural source for the obligation to recite *Malchios*. Rebbi suggests the following: Immediately before the *Yom Tov* of Rosh Hashanah is introduced, at *Leviticus* 23:23, the Torah deals with the obligation to leave פֵּאָה, *a portion of the harvest*, for the poor. The sentence which tells us of this *mitzvah* ends with the words, אֲנִי ה׳ אֱ-לֹהֵיכֶם ..., *I am* HASHEM *your God*. This phrase can be viewed as a springboard from which the *Yom Tov* of Rosh Hashanah is introduced [... אֲנִי ה׳ אֱ-לֹהֵיכֶם ... וּבַחֹדֶשׁ הַשְּׁבִיעִי ...]. It flows in essence from the proposition that God is our Lord — itself the concept of *Malchios* [2].

By making *Pe'ah* the source from which the *Malchios* of Rosh Hashanah are to be derived the Torah clearly wishes to direct our thoughts to that *mitzvah*. All that is implied in the compelling symbolism of this day of days, seems somehow to grow out of the modest requirement that, as we begin to bring in our harvest, we leave a corner of our fields untouched.

Why?

The act of social consciousness which we know as the *mitzvah* of *Pe'ah* has peculiarities which mark it as different from other obligations which devolve upon the farmer such as giving *terumah* to the *Kohen* or *maaser* to the *Levi*.

In these later cases the owner retains some rights [טובת הנאה] in the disposal of his largess. He may give it to whichever *Kohen* or *Levi* he wants, may even, if he feels so inclined, accept money to favor one over the other. He is an active participant, a master, to some extent, of his produce. Certainly there is no question of anyone entering his property and playing fast and loose with his right of way.

Pe'ah is different. We are not to *give* of our harvest to the poor but to *abandon* [תַּעֲזֹב] it to them. They are to enter our fields at will; not as supplicants but as fully entitled proprietors

---

2. Rabbi Yose bar Yehudah adduces a different source — one to which we will return in later essays — this, from *Numbers* 10:10.

functioning at will within the limits which the *halachah* imposes upon them. The owner of the field cannot cast himself as a generous patron of the needy. He is not consulted nor appreciated. He is for all practical purposes — irrelevant.

Such a *mitzvah*, though it disposes of only a negligible percentage of the harvest, cuts away at the very jugular of the untrammeled control with which we normally associate ownership. It testifies unambiguously that nothing, not the bulging granaries which will pour such riches into our coffers, not the vats fat with the wine and oil which will delight our palates, is really our own. *I am* HASHEM *your God!* What you have and what you are comes from My sufferance alone.

That is the *Malchios* of *Pe'ah*.

❈ ❈ ❈

We move back in time to the first Rosh Hashanah — the Friday of creation.

He tested him with a command that should have been easy to obey [. . . וְנִסִיתוֹ בְּמִצְוָה קַלָּה] *but, even that he did not keep.* With this devastating judgment does the *paytan*, in the *pizmon* which we say on *Tzom Gedaliah*, dispose of Adam's failure in Eden. It should not have been hard to abstain from this one fruit when the bounty of the entire garden lay within his grasp. He had everything — save only this. Could he not have been satisfied — and that without undue effort?

If the test to which he was put was indeed a מִצְוָה קַלָּה, an abstention which demanded only minimal self-control, why then did Adam succumb? Are we really to suppose that, with such abundance so easily available, he simply lusted after that particular fruit?

Clearly the struggle lay not in the fruit's physical allure but in the cosmic implications of the prohibition. The apparently insignificant constraint against eating the one, casts its baleful shadow upon the license to enjoy all the others. One small "No!"

robs any "Yes!" of its delight. If God can forbid me the one, then those that are permitted me are only by His sufferance.

Adam was being tested in his willingness to function within the confines of God's *Malchus*. The one fruit which was to be denied him was his *mitzvah* of *pe'ah*. He is not master but servant. He rebelled against the concept of which, one day, David would sing: ... *For all [that we own] we have from You and we have given You only that which comes [to us] from Your hand!*

It was a מִצְוָה קַלָּה, an easy *mitzvah*. But it was terribly hard to keep.

Adam failed. He was driven from Eden because he had spurned the beauty of total subjugation to God. If he is to find his way back it must be through the discovery of *Malchus*.

❧ ❧ ❧

We speak of *Kabolas Ol Malchus Shamayim*, the *shouldering of Heaven's yoke*. A yoke is heavy, irksome and an object of hate. It constricts our liberties, inhibits our movements, frustrates our desires and crushes our individuality.

So we would think.

But paradox of paradoxes! It is not so. Even as a tiny pinprick of a prohibition can, as we saw above, turn into a dreadful burden so too can a potentially oppressive yoke be a source of bliss and contentment. Had Adam been willing to remain unfree he would have earned his freedom. Had he bent his neck to accept heaven's yoke he would have empowered himself to stand straight before His God. Had he subjugated himself to the chaffing and annoying frictions of servitude he would have tasted forever the unalloyed rapture of Eden.

Maharal, *Tiferes Yisrael* 27 is troubled by the fact that the Written Torah does not identify Shavuos as the time of *Mattan Torah*, nor Rosh Hashanah as a day of judgment. We quote his answer:

... This is no problem at all. For God set aside such times for the Holidays as are occasions for joy because of the benefits that accrued to Israel upon them. Thus Pesach is the time that they left Egypt, Succos commemorates their dwelling in booths and Yom Kippur is a day of atonement.

But Shavuos is the day upon which God gave the Torah *which weighs heavy as a yoke* upon the Jews — witness that the other nations refused to accept it. And although we [show our appreciation for having received the Torah by] calling Shavuos, *the day of Mattan Torah*, that is because we willingly accepted it by saying *Na'aseh venishma*. [But that is only from our point of view]. God Himself held the mountain over their heads so that they should be forced to accept the Torah — how then can He [declare a Holiday] ascribing it to the giving of the Torah, when it was He Who imposed it upon us?

It is for this same reason that Rosh Hashanah is not identified as a day of judgment. *Judgment, taken in itself is not something that is gladly shouldered and it is not comfortable for man.* Therefore the Torah does not justify the Holiday on that account but writes only that it is a day of זִכְרוֹן תְּרוּעָה, *a rememberance generated by a [shofar] blast*. Such *rememberance* in common with every time that the term, זְכִירָה is used, always carries a positive connotation. [Note well that *Maharal* seems to differ from *Ramban's* understanding of זָכְרוֹן quoted above.]

Rosh Hashanah, then, appears to be a *Yom Tov* which we have to create ourselves. It is we who have to uncover and discover the joy and satisfaction that can lie in the accountability which is implied in God's judgment. It is we who have to find our way back to the Eden of unquestioning obedience.

היום הרת עולם — *Eternity Conceived*

We began this essay by asking why the *paytan* attaches such importance to the fact that it is *today* that is the birthday of the world; *today* that God calls all His creatures to the bar of justice.

The essence of this Rosh Hashanah harks back to that first Friday of creation. It is on that day — according to the tradition of the Sages, that Adam ate from the Tree of Knowledge, on that day that he shrugged off God's rulership and on that day that he traded the delights of Eden for the eternal fight against the thorn and the thistle.

Rosh Hashanah is the day upon which, by gladly subjugating ourselves to God's judgment we make our own way back to Eden.

אִם כְּבָנִים . . .
Perhaps He Will Look Upon Us As Children

The judge's children, as much as those unrelated to him, must give an accounting for their deeds. But for them the experience is not quite as frightening, the judge's demeanor, not quite as forbidding. The harsh light of truth is softened by compassion, the jagged barbs of guilt are blunted by an understanding born of love: כְּרַחֵם אָב עַל בָּנִים רִחַם ה׳ עַל יְרֵאָיו, *As a father has compassion for his children, so did God have mercy on those who stand in awe of Him* (Psalms 103:13).

How does the judge/father exercise his mercy? What do the eyes, sharpened by love behold, that remains hidden from a less acute vision?

Let us examine the phrase in context.

> . . . Praise HASHEM, O my soul! Never forget all His kindness. He, Who forgives all your sins, Who heals all your illnesses . . . He will not carry a quarrel against you forever, will not bear grudges eternally.
>
> He does not treat us as our sins would warrant, does not punish in accordance with our transgressions . . . As East is far away from West, so has He distanced our rebellions from us.
>
> As a father has compassion for his children, so did God have mercy on those that stand in awe of Him. For He knows our natures, is constantly aware that we are of the dust . . . A wind may pass and already we are no more, forgotten by the very place in which we lived.

היום הרת עולם — *Eternity Conceived*

There is much that we can learn here: Firstly, that God's fatherly mercy is directed specifically towards those that, *stand in awe of Him*. And secondly that His advocacy is compelled by contemplation of man's innate weakness. He understands that we stand vulnerable before the onslaught of our base inclinations [*For He knows our nature*], that we are drawn inexorably downwards because we are of the earth [*... is constantly aware that we are of the dust*], and, above all, that we are no more than sorry weaklings because of our mortality [*... and already we are no more*].

To grasp the implications, we should try to understand — in what sense is God our *father*? From what standpoint can we be considered to be His *children*?

We turn to *Isaiah* 57:16: *For I will not carry a quarrel forever, will not be angry to eternity. For when the spirit is contrite before Me [I recall that] it is I Who made the soul*s.

We quote *Rabbeinu Yonah* in the first *Shaar* of the *Shaarei Teshuvah*:

> The explanation [of the *Isaiah* verse] is: When the spirit which is *before Me*, in that it belongs to that world which is peopled by spiritual creatures [כִּי הוּא מִן הָעֶלְיוֹנִים] suffers the pangs of contrition — then I will no longer quarrel, will not maintain My anger ... For how can I not show limitless compassion for the precious soul which is *before Me* when it is *I Who made the souls*? ... [This latter assertion is based upon the teaching] of our Sages who maintain that there are three partners [each contributing to the forming] of man: His father; his mother; and *HaKadosh Baruch Hu*. Now since father and mother have no part in the soul, it says: *It is I who made the souls*. ...

God, then, is our father — and will look compassionately upon our sincere contrition. This, because as surely as father and mother are our parents because of the physical components which they contribute to our personhood, He too is involved, because of the soul with which He imbues us and which makes us, at least in part, מִן הָעֶלְיוֹנִים.

※ ※ ※

Our *piyut* reads: ... אִם כְּבָנִים אִם כַּעֲבָדִים, *Perhaps He will look upon us as children, perhaps as servants* .... Apparently, then, the father-child relationship with God is not absolute. He may wish to regard us as servants rather than as children.

How so?

Berachos 8a describes how, at death, the soul leaves the body. When the wicked die the break is excruciatingly painful — as difficult as extricating a thorn twig from a tangle of wool. For the righteous the process is easy and painless — the equivalent of lifting a hair from a glass of milk.

The difference is one of identity. Who are we? How are we to be defined in relation to our this-worldly existence and how, to the life of eternity? If the physical in us preponderates, if we have made ourselves absolutely to be creatures of the here and now, then our bodies encompass our essential nature. Our souls must struggle mightily — and agonizingly — to break loose from their cloying embrace. If, on the other hand, we have lived with heart and mind soaring ever upward and onward; if we have cared for our physical needs with the love and respect due a loyal retainer but never permitted ourselves to be conned into a confusion of selfhood; then our bodies and spirits have co-existed, never fused. The moment of separation is sad but painless.

The degree to which God is our father and we, His children, is then determined by our own attitude to life. The more we centralize the physical, the more we subsume our spirits under the sway of the this-worldly and the temporal, the less does our soul retain its affinity to that which He placed within us, to that which made Him an active partner, with our father and mother, in creating us. Conversely, if we have retained mastery over our bodies and lived the balanced life which we described above, then our souls — loci of His fatherhood — have remained untainted and uncompromised — and we can indeed lay claim to being His children.

※ ※ ※

We noted above that God's fatherly mercies are reserved for those who stand in awe of Him and that they are impelled by a willingness to, as it were, distance us from our own failings.

We are now ready to examine each of these two propositions and to understand them in the context of God's fatherhood as we have defined it.

First the matter of awe. Who is it that can truly be said to fear God?

The spirit is lame; the body is blind. This we know from the story which our sages tell in order to illustrate that total man — body and soul together — will one day have to give an accounting before God. The owner of an orchard, unwilling to trust his watchmen to leave the fruit untasted, appointed one who was unable to see — he would never be tempted, and one who was unable to walk — he would lack the means to give in to his cravings. Nothing helped. The lame man sat atop the blind one directing him towards the fruits which he could see but which, on his own, he could never have reached. The owner, when he realized what had occurred, decided to judge them as they had sinned — as one unit. He placed the one atop the other and held them to account.

Thus too will God judge us. Neither the body which on its own cannot see or lust, nor the soul which unaided can gain no access to the forbidden fruits, will be able to claim innocence.

The body, sightless coarse and churlish, knows nothing of awe. It can sniff out danger, it can flee in terror, but it cannot experience the magic of wonder, is not moved by the grandeur of impenetrable mystery. The soul can perceive it, it can intuit the heft and measure of infinity dimly perceived through the prism of its own puniness.

God's children are only those who, with their spiritual acuity uncompromised, can stand in awe before Him.

And for them sin is an aberration. It belongs to the realm of the physical which is far removed from their true essence.

Shabbos 89b tells how in the end of days, God, in despair as it were at Israel's obduracy, will turn to the Patriarchs hoping, as turns out, for their inspired intercession: "Your children have sinned!" He will say to them. Abraham and Jacob, shattered into tragic impotence by this dreadful failing can only declare, "Let them be destroyed so that Your Name may be sanctified!"

God, unhappy with this reaction, will turn to Isaac: Perhaps he will understand what underlies God's plaint, perhaps he will take up the cudgels for his children and find something good to say for Israel. God is not disappointed. In a spirited and impassioned defense Isaac first of all denies God's premise: *"Your children* have sinned!" Why are they his children more than God's, he wants to know. Moreover, he makes God a seemingly strange offer. There are not, he claims, so very many sins about which to worry, and, he implies, God might well consider *bearing* [סבל] these Himself. Should God not wish to do so, he declares himself willing to share the burden. חֲצִי עָלַי וְחֲצִי עָלֶיךָ, he suggests: "Let me carry the half and do You carry the other half!"

There are many questions: Why does Isaac understand what the other two patriarchs do not? What does he mean when he suggests that God Himself might *bear* the sins that were committed? And, above all, what is meant by him and God sharing what has to be borne?

Isaac, more than Abraham or Jacob, is a man of the spirit. He was the עוֹלָה תְּמִימָה, the *unblemished offering* who had been brought up upon God's altar at the *Akeidah*. That experience had effectively shut him off from the realm of the physical. He spent his old age in blindness, closed off from a world to which he could feel no more affinity.

From the vantage point of an Isaac, for one in whom the spiritual preponderates so mightily over the physical, it is possible to view sin as an aberration as, a cruel joke perpetrated by a loutish physicality against the essential goodness of the Jew. And because the body's power to impose its ugly caprices and decadent impulses upon a pure and unwilling soul derives from God Himself it could be argued — and so Isaac did — that God Himself should *bear* the responsibility for the tragic results.

It is a daring concept — but it is not all that Isaac is willing to argue. He himself is also prepared to bear a part of the burden. The blessings which he bestowed upon Eisau fated his children to pass through the terrible centuries of exile. The corrupt influences to which they were thus exposed, no less than the propensity to evil which inheres in human physicality, can readily be blamed for the uneven performance which was now provoking God's anger.

The basis for Isaac's advocacy is thus identical with the thoughts expressed in the Psalm which we examined above. The exercise of God's fatherly mercy expresses itself in a distancing of sin, an awareness of the vulnerability of the frail spirit before the onslaught of brutish passions generated outside the sphere of its own reality, a recognition of just what it means to have been created of the earth.

❦ ❦ ❦

As we invoke God's compassion in the hope that He might regard us as children rather than as servants, we would do well to remember that we can project ourselves as children only so long as we comport ourselves in a way that God would be willing to recognize us as His own. He imbued our physical bodies with the breath of His own being. If it is this נְשָׁמָה, this *product of God's own essence* [נְשָׁמָה, derives from, נשם, *to breathe*] which defines our being — then we can be confident that He will *have mercy upon us as a father would over his children.*

אִם כַּעֲבָדִים . . . ❧
Perhaps He Will Look Upon Us As Servants

Even if we do not merit the compassion [רַחֲמִים – כְּרַחֵם אָב עַל בָּנִים. . .] which a father would show a child, we may still hope for the freely bestowed grace [. . . חֲנִינָה – . . . עַד שֶׁתְּחָנֵּנוּ] by which a master might be willing to help the vulnerable and the weak — the servant who can look to no one else for succor.

Our phrase is borrowed from *Psalm* 123, and, so that we may grasp as much of its import as possible, we should quote it in full.

> . . . To You, Who dwell in heaven I lift up my eyes. See! They are like the eyes of servants looking towards their master, like the eyes of a maid-servant looking towards her mistress, so are our eyes [turned] to HASHEM our God in the hope that He will grant us grace [עַד שֶׁיְחָנֵּנוּ]. O HASHEM show us abundant grace [חָנֵּנוּ ה' חָנֵּנוּ] because we have been overwhelmed by derision. We have been overwhelmed with the derision of those who dwell in tranquility, with the contempt of the arrogant.

Apparently *freely bestowed grace* constitutes the particular hope of the helpless and the hopeless — the slave.

❧ ❧ ❧

We have rendered the root חנן as denoting, *freely bestowed grace*. This on the basis of *Sifrey*, *Va'Eschanan* 6 [quoted in *Rashi* to *Deuteronomy* 3:23]: Wherever חַנּוּן is used, it denotes, מַתְּנַת חִנָּם, *a freely bestowed gift*, one that is not prompted by any sense of obligation.

An עֶבֶד, a *slave* has no right to expect his master's forbearance. He is an instrument — not a discrete entity, a means — never a self-justifying end. There is no room for רַחֲמִים [related to רֶחֶם, the *womb*, and therefore connoting a feeling of love and warmth growing out of kinship] here. Clemency, if shown at all, will be rooted in the master's purpose, not in the servants claim.

❀ ❀ ❀

Let us consider our own עֶבֶד relationship with God. In what sense are we His servants? What might justify us in anticipating his חֲנִינָה?

To gain some insight into the nature of this relationship we would do well to examine *Shiras Haazinu*, that final legacy of Moshe Rabbeinu which, when read with care and sensitivity can yield the keys to the understanding of our entire history.

It is in many ways a sad document. It talks of failures, backslidings and disloyalties, of consequent suffering and estrangement and almost — total rejection. But, withal, it ends on a triumphant note of reconciliation.

It is instructive to trace the expressions which *Haazinu* uses to describe Israel in the context of its failings: They were his *children*. Their backsliding harmed them, not Him (32:5); Is He not your *father* who created you . . . (32:6); You have undermined the rock *Who bore you*, have forgotten the Almighty *Who brought you forth* (32:18); . . . they are *children* whom one cannot trust (32:20).

Invariably we are described as children who have fallen short of that which was expected of them.

When *Haazinu* moves into the reconciliation stage, we are immediately struck by a significant change: When HASHEM will judge His people, He will look mercifully upon *His servant* (32:36); O you nations sing songs of jubilation to His people, for He will avenge the blood of His *servants* (32:43).

What brought about the change of imagery from *children* to *servants*?

The transition appears to have been set in motion by v.26: *I had intended to leave them unprotected, to wipe out their memory from among man*. [I would indeed have done this] *were it not that I feared the fury of the foe, that their enemies might be mislead, that they might say, "Our own strength was overpowering, it is not God Who wrought all this"*.

This verse, as *Ramban* understands it holds the key to the enigma of Jewish survival in the face of the constant failings and disappointments which make up so much of our history.

We quote *Ramban* in full:

> [The statement that God had wanted to destroy us refers] to our present exile ... in which, if absolute justice were to hold sway, we would have to remain forever were it not for the *fury of the foe*. This indicates that in our present situation there is nothing left of the *merit of the fathers* [תַּמָּה זְכוּת אָבוֹת] and we can hope for salvation only in the merit of God's great name. This in accordance with numerous passages in the prophets in which it is stated clearly that God will help us in our exile not because we deserve it but only to avoid the desecration of His name. It is for this reason that Moses, in his prayer, said: "Then the nations which have heard of Your fame might say ..." And God agreed with this argument and answered: "I have decided to forgive *in accordance with that which you have said* [סָלַחְתִּי כִּדְבָרֶיךָ]."
>
> Now the sense of this phrase is by no means that it expresses a desire to flaunt His strength to His enemies, for all the people are as nothing to Him, they are utterly worthless in His eyes. But [God's consideration was based on the fact that] He had created a physical world so that humans might recognize Him and adore Him. But — He granted them absolute freedom. They may choose to do either good or evil. Now when mankind

chose freely to sin and to deny Him, only this one nation [Israel] remained true to Him. Through the miracles which accompanied them throughout their history, He made it known that He is the One Omnipotent God — and this became known to all the nations.

Now if God should ever decide to destroy them, then all the nations would forget all these miracles and no one would ever mention them again. And even if they would occasionally come to mind, people would ascribe all these occurrences to natural causes with no current significance. Thus would the entire purpose of creation be undermined for no one would remember God meaningfully, but on the contrary, people would only anger Him.

Therefore *the very will which prompted God to create the world in the first place, must guarantee that Israel remain His people eternally. For it is they alone, among all the nations, who are close to Him and who have an accurate perception of Him.*

Now that is the meaning of the verse, *When* HASHEM *will judge His people, He will look mercifully upon His servant* (there v.36). The meaning is that God will in His mercy recall that they are His servants who remained true to Him throughout their exile, loyally bearing the burdens of suffering and slavery ...

In the context of our discussion, the final paragraph is particularly significant: The meaning is that God will in His mercy recall *that they are His servants* who remained true to Him throughout their exile, loyally bearing the burdens of suffering and slavery ...

The *servant* relationship then is determined by a willingness to shoulder the terrible burdens of loyalty, to continue as instrument of the master's purpose even during those dark periods during which no sense of personal connectedness inspires and the loving concern of the father has been usurped by callous, cruel, uncaring history.

※ ※ ※

Rav Wolbe, in his Alei Shur talks of יְמֵי אַהֲבָה and יְמֵי שִׂנְאָה, *days of adoration* when all seems well in our relationship to God, when we bask in the warmth of love and certainty and know ourselves to be cradled in God's arms; and *days of aversion* or alienation when we experience nothing but loneliness and despair.

Our *paytan* knows this well and understands that we cannot always hope to enjoy the *mercy* which a child expects from his father. But even when we feel most abandoned we can, with determination and grit, remain God's *servants*. We can dream His dreams, hope His hopes and live lives which are a projection of His will. None of this will give us a claim upon Him. A servant deserves no credit for — serving. But, for loyalty maintained through darkness and distance there is an unlimited fount of חֲנִינָה, of *freely bestowed grace*, which may yet give us hope.

זָכְרֵנוּ לְחַיִּים מֶלֶךְ חָפֵץ בַּחַיִּים,
וְכָתְבֵנוּ בְּסֵפֶר הַחַיִּים,
לְמַעַנְךָ אֱלֹהִים חַיִּים.

Remember us for life,
O King Who desires life,
and inscribe us in the Book of Life —
for Your sake, O Living God.

מִי כָמוֹךָ אַב הָרַחֲמִים,
זוֹכֵר יְצוּרָיו לְחַיִּים בְּרַחֲמִים.

Who is like You, Merciful Father,
Who recalls His creatures mercifully for life!

וּכְתוֹב לְחַיִּים טוֹבִים כָּל בְּנֵי בְרִיתֶךָ.

And inscribe all the children of Your covenant
for a good life.

בְּסֵפֶר חַיִּים בְּרָכָה וְשָׁלוֹם,
וּפַרְנָסָה טוֹבָה,
נִזָּכֵר וְנִכָּתֵב לְפָנֶיךָ
אֲנַחְנוּ וְכָל עַמְּךָ בֵּית יִשְׂרָאֵל,
לְחַיִּים טוֹבִים וּלְשָׁלוֹם.

In the book of life, blessing, and peace,
and good livelihood,
may we be remembered and inscribed before You —
we and Your entire people the Family of Israel
for a good life and for peace.

זָכְרֵנוּ לְחַיִּים . . . ◆§
Remember Us for Life . . .

The insertion of this little prayer at this particular place jangles the senses. We are inserting a בַּקָּשָׁה, an *entreaty*, in a context in which it seems to have no legitimate standing. R' Chaninah taught: The [first three blessings] have the character of a servant extolling his master's praises; the middle [blessings] have the character of a servant begging his master for his needs; the last [three blessings] have the character of a servant who having had his needs filled by his master leaves [his master's] presence and departs (*Berachos* 34a).

The legitimate place for entreaty is thus not in the first grouping nor in the last, but only in the middle blessings.[1]

Our carping is justified by more than the apparent aesthetic disharmony. The precisely limited functions of the first and last groupings which seem to leave no room at all for the making of any requests are firmly embedded in the *halachah*: Rav Yehudah taught: No one should ever ask for his needs [to be filled] in either the first three or the last three [blessings] (*Berachos*, there).

How, then, to explain our usage?

Indeed, our problem occasioned a great deal of controversy in the *Gaonic* literature. *Rav Hai Gaon*, for example, reports that in at least one of the great Babylonian Yeshivos it was not the custom to make any insertions.

Nevertheless, he himself, and, in greater detail, *Rav Tzemach Gaon* (or, according to some records, *Rav Kohen Tzedek*)

---

1. Of the three companion phrases only the third presents the same degree of difficulty. The second, . . . מִי כָמוֹךָ is an exclamation of praise, not a petition. The fourth, . . . בְּסֵפֶר חַיִּים occurs in the last blessing, . . . שִׂים שָׁלוֹם itself couched in the form of an entreaty. Only the third, . . . וּכְתוֹב seems as incongruous as the first.

36 / A MACHZOR COMPANION

construct a justification. It is possible to differentiate between personal needs [צָרְכֵי יָחִיד] which are clearly interdicted under Rav Yehudah's ruling, and communal needs [צָרְכֵי צִבּוּר] against which there are no *halachic* strictures. *Zochreinu*, couched as it is in the plural, is a prayer that God grant life to everyone and ought thus to be viewed as expressing a communal need.

The *Gaonim* feel that this difference can be maintained on the basis of textual analysis. Rav Yehudah did not say, . . . אֵין שׁוֹאֲלִין, *One may not ask* . . . — which would have implied a blanket constraint — but, . . . אַל יִשְׁאַל אָדָם צְרָכָיו, *Let a man not ask for* his *needs*, which apparently limits the objection to those of the individual. Moreover, they point out, that the first and third blessings of the second grouping are cast in the form of requests — *May our service find acceptance* . . . , and *Grant peace* . . . . And this can only be reconciled with Rav Yehudah's proscription if we postulate the suggested distinction.

We have discovered the rationalization upon which our usage is based, but we have not explained it. Why are communal needs different? Why do the former not offend against the *praise* content of these blessings?

Tur, Orach Chaim 112 offers an explanation: The fact that an entire community stands in need of God's benevolence is eloquent testimony to His omnipotence. The admission of absolute dependence which inheres in our entreaty that God grant our communal needs stands in seamless consonance with the *praise* character of the blessing.

This rationalization appears first in a responsum by *Rabbeinu Tam* quoted in *Shibbolei HaLeket, Tefillah* 28, and was then appropriated by *Rosh* to *Berachos*. From there it found its way into the *Tur* and into subsequent *halachic* works.

The *Gaonim* themselves do not offer this explanation. Indeed, from one phrase which occurs in their writings, they appear to have had an altogether different concept in mind.

Indeed the very concept which seems to animate the explanation offered by *Rabbeinu Tam* and *Rosh*, the idea that this petition forms an integral part of the blessings in which it appears, seems contradicted by our own sense of aesthetics. For, even if we grant that God's glory is somehow enhanced by communal dependence upon His goodwill, we still cannot comfortably maintain that this *praise* is of a piece with the content of the first blessing. The sense that life depends on God — the thought which compels the entreaty that God *remember us for life* — does not really belong within a context which speaks of history [*Avos*] and Messianic promise [*... and brings redemption to their descendants ...*].

Again we are hard put to appreciate the idea that somehow communal dependence enhances God's glory more than does the fact that every individual too must turn to Him in his hour of need.

It seems possible that the *Gaonim* who first suggested the difference between communal and individual needs did not want to find a formula which would defend the *integration* of the *zochreinu* prayer within the first blessing, but, were, on the contrary, bent on justifying blatant and aesthetically offensive *disjunction*. Its very discordant stridency jumps *out* of the text, and forces us to pay attention.

We spoke before of a phrase which appears in the *Gaonic* responsa and which, we feel, confirms our perception. After making the point that communal needs may be judged by different criteria than are those of the individual, *Rav Tzemach Gaon* ends with the words, וְהַשָּׁעָה צְרִיכָה לְכָךְ, *... and it is the need of the moment!* The implication is clear. There is no real justification for placing this entreaty in a contextual environment in which it clearly does not belong. It is there because there is no choice. First aid administered at the scene of an accident pays scant heed to the cosmetic considerations which, in other circumstances, might be appropriate.

The very incongruence of the positioning turns a conventional prayer into a scream for help. What we are really doing when we beg God for life in the first blessing is to say: There is no time now for the niceties of etiquette. Our desperation must crash the barriers of convention. We should, O God, sing Your praises before we importune you with our petty needs. But we cannot wait. Let us live, let us only live, and we will then once more pick up the appropriate forms of address and prayer. But — first and above all: Let us live!

We turn to *Sefer HaPardes*, a *halachic* compendium stemming from *Rashi's* school, and find that this is precisely how he understood the *Gaonim's* idea. Because of the extreme significance of the passage which goes beyond our immediate concern and focuses on the much broader issue of communal prayer תְּפִילַת הַצִּבּוּר, we provide a loose translation.

> Rav Yehudah's ruling that we are not to offer entreaties in the first three and final three blessings is limited to an individual who wishes to give voice to his own needs. But if one such would pray for the community, and, it goes without saying, if the community utters prayers for the community — then this is not interdicted under Rav Yehudah's ruling.
>
> In support of this assertion we can cite *Yerushalmi* (*Berachos* 4:4): When we invite a *chazan* to represent us in prayer we do not say to him, "Come pray! [בּוֹא וְהִתְפַּלֵל]," but we say, "Come, draw near! Present our sacrifice! Fill our needs! Wage war for us! Elicit good-will!" Now the fact that we do not say to him, "Come pray [בּוֹא וְהִתְפַּלֵל]" proves that communal prayer does not require that petition be preceded by praise. No formalities are necessary. God's attention is immediate and unmediated.
>
> It can be demonstrated that this is the meaning of *Yerushalmi's* assertion that we do not say, "Come

pray". The word תְּפִילָה, *prayer*, connotes the *extolling of praises*. Witness the teaching recorded in *Avodah Zarah* 7b: *Let a man pray*, יִתְפַּלֵּל, *and only then petition for the fulfillment of his needs*. Clearly then if we do not demand that the communities' representative *pray*, this means that we do not require him to precede his petitions with praise.

הֶן אֵ-ל כַּבִּיר וְלֹא יִמְאָס, *God will never treat the overpowering force* [כַּבִּיר] *of communal need lightly*. They possess an energy which those of an individual can never equal.

HaPardes's perception of the *Gaonim's* differentiation is clear. Communal prayer packs such weight and import that it may dispense with normal etiquette. No barriers exist. The community may demand — and God is receptive to their importuning whether or not it is couched in an appropriate form. The entreaty that God grant us life has no place in the first blessing. It pushes aside whatever it perceives as irrelevant to the urgency of its needs. It brooks no delay — it demands to be heard.

It transpires that *HaPardes's* perception of the *Gaonim's* ruling is the very opposite of that of *Rosh* and *Rabbeinu Tam*. His ear picks up discord, not harmony. And the pathos of the plea lies in just that dissonance. Whoever ordained that *zochreinu* be recited in the first blessing was telling us that the petition for life during the *Asseres Yemei Teshuvah* is serious business.

❦ ❦ ❦

כְּדַלִּים וּכְרָשִׁים דָּפַקְנוּ דְלָתֶיךָ, *We knock at Your door as though we were indigents, as those who have nothing at all*. This is how we present ourselves to God at the start of our *Selichos* prayers. We are comfortable with assuming the stance of the mendicant. We know — O how we know! — that we have no rights, no merits with which to face our Creator. It make sense that we should throw ourselves upon His mercies. They are true and they are tried. From us — we know it — they will not be withheld.

And yet — prayer holds other possibilities.

Choni HaMe'agel's demand that God grant rain to His famished people before he would release himself from the famous circle within which he had caged himself was not the timid knock of the supplicant. It was the self-assured insistence of one who knows that God *must* answer. There simply is no alternative.

When the men of Nineveh were shocked into repentance by Yonah, they *cried to God with brazen conviction* [וַיִּקְרְאוּ אֶל־אֱ-לֹהִים בְּחָזְקָה]. Our Sages wonder what this expression might mean. Their interpretation rattles our certainties: חֲצִיפָה נָצַח לְבִישָׁה, כָּל שֶׁכֵּן לְטוֹבָתוֹ שֶׁל עוֹלָם, *Arrogance overpowers timidity — most certainly when He Who has the good of the world at heart is concerned* (Pesikat d'Rav Kahana, Shuvah). As simple as that! The strong, the assured, the self-confident will get his way. This is true when he is pitted against man, it is doubly true when he is pitted, as it were, against God.

We quote *Ramban* to *Exodus* 13:12.

> ... Our purpose in raising our voice in prayer, the reason why we pray in synagogues, *the merit that accrues from communal prayer* — all that is for this; that people should have a place wherein they might gather and thank God for having created them and for having brought them forth, that they might announce this in public, declaring to Him: "We owe our existence to You!"
>
> This is what the Sages meant when they interpreted the verse from *Yonah* to teach that prayer should be spoken loudly, for *arrogance overpowers timidity* ...

Ramban appears to confirm out thesis. The very nature of communal prayer is a form of brashness. It arrogates to itself the right to demand — because the need is compelling. There is no other way.

Particularly in the *Aseres Yemei Teshuvah* does this hold true. As R' *Tzemach Gaon* writes, *the time demands it*. The niceties of opening our prayers with God's praises are appropriate to other times, to other situations. When our very existence hangs in the balance we crash in to God's presence without formality — and know, deep down, that we will be answered.

מִי כָמוֹךָ אַב הָרַחֲמִים ... ১৯
Who Is Like You Merciful Father ...

We noted in the previous essay that this insertion does not present the same problem as does *zochreinu* ... in the earlier blessing. It is clearly formulated as an exclamation of *praise* and accordingly it does not offend against the tenor of the first three blessings.

Our task is rather to analyze whether there is any natural linkage between the recognition of God's *mercy* and the particular Divine attributes of which this second blessing speaks.

Megillah 17a calls this blessing, גְּבוּרוֹת, that is, that it lauds the *might* which God demonstrates in His mastery of the world. *Might* expresses itself in unfettered dominion over the otherwise immutable laws of nature. God, in untrammeled freedom undeterred by what "ought" to be, supports that which by any known criteria should fall, heals those who really have no expectation of life and frees the utterly hopeless from their bonds. Even the most absolute of nature's decrees — that that which has died can never live again — does not inhibit Him. He *brings the dead alive in abundant mercy*.

Does this context provide a natural home for our, ... מִי כָמוֹךָ? Does the idea that God is unique as the *Merciful father Who in great compassion grants life to those whom He has formed* belong together with a listing of the instances in which Divine fiat defies natural law?

R' Moshe Chaim Luzzatto in the fourth chapter of his *Mesillas Yesharim* makes the point that God's love of מִשְׁפָּט, *absolute justice*, assures that He will not overlook even the smallest infraction of the law. We quote:

זכרנו לחיים — *Remember Us for Life* / 43

> ... For it must be understood that a leniency which condones faults stands in contradiction to the concept of מִשְׁפָּט as much as would the ignoring of merit. Therefore ... it is necessary that God react to our actions, both good and bad, with absolute precision ... that He demand an accurate accounting, and that he punish even the smallest sin. There simply can be no escape.

If then, מִשְׁפָּט demands such stern and unyielding exactitude, we are hard put to find a legitimation for the exercise of mercy. Do the two ideas, *justice* and *mercy* not stand in contradiction to one another?

Mesilas Yesharim tackles this question and, after postulating that not only is God merciful but that the quality of mercy literally sustains the world which could not hope to exist without it, he delimits its function to three areas in such a way that the concept of justice is not affronted:

> ... This, because pure justice would demand that the sinner be punished immediately upon sinning without any respite at all. Also, that the punishment be prompted by an absolute fury [and therefore be extremely harsh] as befits one who has rebelled against his Creator. And that the sin, once committed, should stand without any hope that it might be forgiven. How, after all, is it possible to eradicate the past? What is done, is done.
>
> However, mercy decrees the opposite of these three demands: That the sinner be given time; that the punishment be a measured one so that he will not be destroyed; and that, as an act of pure kindness [on God's part], he be given the option of repentance, that the elimination of the will-to-sin be considered as an elimination [retroactively] of the sin itself ...

> ... Now none of these three leniencies can be said to be appropriate in a mode of pure justice — but nevertheless they also do not stand in contradiction to it. For there is a certain logic for allowing the agony of regret to be accepted as atonement for the ecstasy of the sin. The granting of time for the sinner to come to his senses is also not a condoning of the sin, being no more than a little exercise in patience ...

Apparently then, the demands of justice must be met, but they are not inflexible. A certain elasticity prevails. It is, after all, possible to substitute will-to-sin for the sin to create an ambience within which *teshuvah* becomes possible, to have pain atone for pleasure and to exercise some restraint in the execution of that which must ultimately be done.

It is possible. But is the reasoning compelling? Are we not simply begging the question by softening its contours? If, for example, *absolute justice* demands immediate reprisal, are we not compromising its exacting standards by allowing for patience?

Our unease dissipates when we examine more closely the place of *mishpat* within the total scheme of God's stewardship of human affairs.

We turn to another of *Luzzattos's* works, the *Derech HASHEM* chapter 8.

> ... Now we know well that God's only wish is to do the best for us. It is also clear that He loves us as a father loves his children.
>
> But — love itself demands that a father punish his son to the latter's eternal benefit.
>
> ... From this it transpires that justice and the law themselves grow from a source of love. The punishment which God inflicts does not flow from vengeance or enmity, but is the loving discipline to which a caring father subjects his son.

We derive two principles from this insight: Firstly that the punishment itself is softened, never harsh or cruel. This, because love itself guarantees that justice be tempered by mercy. Secondly, that occasionally, as circumstances demand, God may forgo justice altogether and permit Himself to be motivated only by mercy ...

When we talk of God's loving us [אָבִינוּ] and, at the same time, His treating us with firm and demanding discipline [מַלְכֵּנוּ] we do not imply that the two characteristics are coequal. The essential component of God's relationship to us is love and only love. He is first father and only then, king. Justice is a subordinate value which is necessitated by love and thus, contoured by love. It has neither intrinsic nor independent standing. While justice is a fundamental attribute it yields to the fatherly mercy which allows for *Teshuvah*.

Mesilas Yesharim's thesis thus becomes easy to understand. We were troubled by the fact that mercy, in the three manifestations which he assigned to it, still appeared to be an affront to מִשְׁפָּט in its purest form. The answer is that, indeed, the two are ultimately incompatible — but it does not matter. There is no need for justice to be absolute since it functions as no more than a facilitator for an agenda much larger than itself. It need be no more perfect than is required to remain in consonance with love's goals.

The logic is clear, the problem seems solved — but we are left vaguely unsatisfied. Our instincts rebel against a conception of מִשְׁפָּט as anything less than an essential component of God's relationship with man. Particularly during the *Aseres Yemei Teshuvah* when we substitute the stern הַמֶּלֶךְ הַמִּשְׁפָּט, *the King Whose very essence is justice* for the much softer, מֶלֶךְ אוֹהֵב צְדָקָה וּמִשְׁפָּט, *the King Who loves charity and justice* does the thought appear to be incongruous. Moreover, *justice* [מִשְׁפָּט] is certainly rooted in *truth* [אֱמֶת]. And we ask ourselves: "Is a compromised truth, true? Can אֱמֶת ever be anything less than absolute? If אֱמֶת/מִשְׁפָּט demands a punishment that is immediate and harsh, is not anything which falls short of that standard — שֶׁקֶר, a *sham*?"

On Rosh Hashanah we meet the *God of Truth*: כִּי אַתָּה אֱלֹהִים אֱמֶת וּדְבָרְךָ אֱמֶת וְקַיָּם לָעַד . . ., *For You are the true God and Your word is true and endures forever* . . . . Is there room for *mercy* on such a day?

Here, it would seem, the exercise of Divine mercy intersects with the גְּבוּרָה of which the second blessing speaks. In order to be the *Merciful father Who in great compassion grants life to those whom He has formed*, God must, as it were, struggle against the demands of an uncompromising truth which, in and from its very essence, must spurn any softening as a compromise of the very integrity which is its life-blood. God's love must, as it were, overcome the anguished protests of an אֱמֶת which must submissively yield to that love.

During the *Aseres Yemei Teshuvah* God answers for all of us the prayer of R' Yismael the High Priest "May it be Your will that Your mercy conquer Your anger" (*Berachos* 7a). We praise God for, so to speak, mastering Himself even as He masters the mighty forces of nature.

※ ※ ※

There may be another explanation for the inclusion of *mi komocha* in this particular blessing.

We learned from the *Mesilas Yesharim* that one aspect of God's mercy is His willingness to allow the sinner to eradicate his guilt through *teshuvah*. It is indeed a radical idea — one which militates against the concept of time which is so firmly implanted in our consciousness. The past is gone, the act has been committed — it should, by any logic be beyond retrieval. And yet, Torah and tradition tell us that it is not so. Let the sinner but repent seriously, let him determine to break the shackles of the past, let him in earnest contrition confess his wrong-doing — and the slate is wiped clean. More! If his *teshuvah* is motivated by love [תְּשׁוּבָה מֵאַהֲבָה] his very rebellions will be turned retroactively to merits. Against all expectations the fist of *teshuvah* smashes the barriers of time, projects the present into the past — and in defiant disregard of the rational and the reasonable produces the miracle of absolute atonement.

Mesilas Yesharim's rationalization that the mechanics of *teshuvah* have a certain logic of their own, that it is possible to substitute the will-to-sin for the sin itself, is just that — a rationalization. It explains the "how" of *teshuvah* but not the "why." It does not obviate the shattering implications of a process which finds its natural environment in a state of beyond-time.

Indeed, it would seem that the possibility to do *teshuvah* draws upon God's mercies. Without them the idea is inconceivable (see *Shaarei Teshuvah* 1:1).

And yet — this proposition requires analysis. To our intense surprise it is not only sin that can be retroactively eradicated, but also merit.

Based on *Ezekiel* 33:12, *The righteousness of the righteous one shall not save him on the day of his iniquity ...*, *Kiddushin* 40b asserts that reward for *mitzvos* performed is contingent upon a continued identification with the motives which originally prompted them. If a person were ever to regret having performed a given *mitzvah* [תוהה על הראשונות], then his *righteousness shall not save him*.

Apparently then, we are able to do "*teshuvah*" for *mitzvos* performed, as much as for sins committed. The former are eradicated as effectively as the latter. Such harsh rejection of a conscientiously performed *mitzvah* is certainly not rooted in God's mercies.

But why is our earlier analysis incorrect? How can today's attitudes affect — positively or negatively — the actions of yesterday?

Many thinkers have grappled with this issue.

Rav Hutner offers a simple explanation.

There is a vast difference between regretting having performed a *mitzvah* and repenting for an earlier transgression. That difference is rooted in the well established coupling of the two concepts, *mitzvah*/life and sin/death.

Life needs to be nurtured. We must breathe, we must eat, we must do all those things upon which life is conditioned.

Death is absolute. Nothing is needed to sustain it. It is the ultimate negative. It is *not* being. It is dreadfully final.

The performance of a *mitzvah* grants life. But the nurture and sustaining force of that life must grow from an appreciation of the sanctity [... אֲשֶׁר קִדְּשָׁנוּ בְּמִצְוֹתָיו] which the *mitzvah* has generated. That is its food, that, its breath of life. Absent such appreciation, the life withers, the energy flags, and in the end nothing at all will be left. The process is a natural one and should elicit no surprise.

No such prosaic normalcy can be invoked to explain the vivifying efficacy of *teshuvah* upon the sin-generated death of the sinner. Such a process, a veritable resurrection, partakes of the miraculous and can only be explained in terms of God's unbounded mercy.

As such, a reflection upon God as the One Who *in great compassion grants life to those whom He has formed* has its natural home in the blessing of תְּחִיַּת הַמֵּתִים.

וּכְתוֹב לְחַיִּים טוֹבִים כָּל בְּנֵי בְרִיתֶךָ
Inscribe All Those With Whom You Have Forged Your Covenant For a Good Life

The petition seems straightforward enough. Nevertheless there are nuances which signal clearly that all is not as simple as it seems. Why חַיִּים טוֹבִים, a *good life* as opposed to simply חַיִּים, *life*, as in the first two insertions? Why בְּנֵי בְרִיתֶךָ, *All those with whom You have forged Your covenant* instead of simply, *us* as in the first and fourth insertions, or *those Whom You have created* as in the second?[1]

First, a digression in which we analyze the meaning of, חַיִּים as it is used in this blessing. Why וְכֹל הַחַיִּים יוֹדוּךָ סֶּלָה, . . . *all those who live will thank You to all eternity* rather than simply, *everybody*? There is no question of such a usage being accidental. It is, of course, axiomatic that every word was carefully weighed by the Sages who gave our prayers form and body. But, beyond that, the stress on *life* in a blessing which has as its focus our gratitude to God for all the wonders which He has done for us is attested in our בִּרְכַּת הַמָּזוֹן. There, the second blessing, . . . נוֹדֶה לְךָ, parallels our . . . מוֹדִים and the choice of its terminology is striking

---

1. *Machzor Vitri* (p.366) cites a custom according to which the first insertion is to read, זָכְרֵנוּ לְחַיִּים טוֹבִים . . . וְכָתְבֵנוּ בְּסֵפֶר חַיִּים טוֹבִים and lauds it as appropriate. For those who do not have this reading he offers two justifications, the first in the name of *Rabbeinu Tam*: The *Aseres Yemei Teshuvah* are a time of good-will [עֵת רָצוֹן] and God would not bestow His largess half-heartedly. If we pray for *life* He will, of His own accord, grant us a *good life*.

For the second, he cites *Rashi*. Prayer ought constantly to widen one's expectations. Thus in the first insertion we ask simply for life; in the second petition [that is the third insertion] we ask for a good life; and in the last for a good life accompanied by peace [לְחַיִּים טוֹבִים וּלְשָׁלוֹם].

Our question assumes *Rabbeinu Tam's* position.

indeed. . . . יִתְבָּרַךְ שִׁמְךָ בְּפִי כָּל חַי, *May Your name be blessed by the mouth of all living [creatures].*

We follow Rav Hutner in his analysis of the place which הַכָּרַת הַטוֹב, *the sense of awareness that undeserved kindnesses were bestowed and of the responsibilities which accrue from being a recipient of such favors*, an awareness which, in English we express by the bland and non-evocative word *gratitude*, plays in the thought-world of the Torah.

His point of departure is *Proverbs* 15:27 which teaches that, שׂוֹנֵא מַתָּנוֹת יִחְיֶה, *Only he is truly alive who hates to accept presents.*

Rav Hutner notes that in Hebrew we speak of well-water as מַיִם חַיִּים, *living water*. *Life* is thus equated with independence; it sparkles with a determination and an ability to be self-sustaining and self-replenishing. Dependence, lack of self-sufficiency, wanting, grasping, begging, jealousy, covetousness, the famished heart — all these bespeak a kind of spiritual limbo, a non-life, drab, sad and ultimately self-destroying.

But man is never completely self-sufficient. Our natural life plays itself out as part of a society in which we take as well as give, ask as well as grant, interact happily and productively, contributing but also drawing out, each of us both benefactor and beneficiary.

Are we then condemned to spiritual sterility? If taking is death — how shall we live?

It is here that הַכָּרַת הַטוֹב steps in. It transforms an act of taking into one of giving, transposes the roles in the transaction, and can leave the donor more enriched than the recipient of his largess. The one hands the other a piece of bread — and he is rewarded with the warm glow of appreciation which has a value beyond gold. Let him who by circumstances is forced to accept a favor but bring himself to say, and more importantly to feel, a heartfelt thanks and he will belong into the ranks of those *who hate to accept presents.*

This thought, we feel, informs the terminology of which we spoke above. In both our blessings it is the *living* who sing God's praises. In bowing low before God they become God-like, givers instead of takers, active and vital instead of passive and constricted. It is a craving for life which animates them.

I bow, therefore I am!

※ ※ ※

There is a paradox here. Self-abnegation turns into self-assertion, the rounded spine becomes symbol of a straight back. We should analyze the extent to which this paradox informs the spirit of the *modim* blessing, what it says to us about our relationship to God.

Sotah 40a poses a question which, at first sight, we are hard-put to understand: What do the people say while the *shliach tzibbur* recites *modim*? Rav answers, מוֹדִים אֲנַחְנוּ לָךְ ה׳ אֱלֹ־הֵינוּ עַל שֶׁאָנוּ מוֹדִים לָךְ, *We thank you* HASHEM, *our God — for thanking You*. Other *amoraim* suggest other wordings and it is from a combination of the various opinions that our *modim de'Rabanan* is compiled.

What assumptions underlay the Gemara's question? Why would the people say anything at all while the *shliach tzibbur* recites *modim* any more than they say anything during the other blessings? What is the meaning, and what are the implications, of Rav's answer?

Rashi explains his formulation as follows: [We thank You] for having inspired us to cleave to You and to thank You.

The implications are enormous. Nothing is our own — not even our thank-yous. The most destitute of mendicants, in his relationship to his benefactor, is richer by far than we as we stand before God. He owns nothing, is beholden for the clothes on his emaciated back, the mean crust which keeps body and soul together — but he remains a man, free and unbowed. He is able to bestow the most precious of gifts upon the person who helped him — the gift of gratitude. We have nothing, nothing at all. The very feelings which move us, the sense of obligation which marks us as responsible humans — and in which, consequently, we might have taken some pride, all this comes to us from God. He is the source of our inspiration; we are nothing, nothing and once more, nothing.

Rav's insight came as a result of the Gemara's question: What do the people say while the *shliach tzibbur* recites *modim*? We must now make an attempt to understand this question.

Megillah 18a discusses the sequence in which the blessings of the *amidah* prayer are organized. In explaining why ... רְצֵה precedes ... מוֹדִים the Gemara formulates the principle that, עֲבוֹדָה וְהוֹדָאָה חֲדָא מִילְתָא הִיא, *Divine service* [עֲבוֹדָה, the content of רְצֵה] *is as one with the expression of thanks* [הוֹדָאָה, the content of מוֹדִים]. The two ideas are a part of an integrated whole. Gratitude grows from an awareness of dependence, is itself an expression of the servitude which derives from such dependence. Gratitude speaks of beholdenness, it is ultimately an admission of inadequacy. [ידה, the root of מוֹדֶה, *to thank* is also the root of מוֹדֶה, *to admit*. The two are ideationally related. When I thank, I admit that by myself I could not have attained that which I needed to attain, that I needed the other to put me on my feet. It creates obligation, and obligation makes me unfree, it impresses me into servitude (*Rav Hutner*)]

Such absolute submission cannot be accomplished by proxy. The congregation must join in, must — personally — affirm their subjection. What, the Gemara wonders, is appropriate for them to say? What can best express their acquiescence to the *shliach tzibbur's* מוֹדִים?

Rav's solution is that they must go even further. The *shliach tzibbur* renders thanks for favors received, they render thanks for the ability to render thanks. They declare themselves to be empty vessels — nothing of their own, nothing at all.

❊ ❊ ❊

זכרנו לחיים — *Remember Us for Life* / 53

We have, as it were, painted ourselves into a corner. We had thought that the feeling of gratitude has the redeeming function of transforming an act of taking into an act of giving, that we speak of the חַיִּים who give thanks because it is the expression of thanks which allows entry into the ranks of those who *hate to accept presents*.

But does not Rav's contention serve to vitiate our thesis? If even our *thank you* is a gift from God then, once more, we are no more than passive receivers. Our lives are non-lives, a pathetic charade which cloaks — nothing.

We conclude that, indeed, the חַיִּים of which we speak in this blessing is not a *good life*, a חַיִּים טוֹבִים. It is, so to speak, a life by sufferance. It is true that even our thanks are inspired by God — but they are only *inspired*. It is we who react to the inspiration, it is we who formulate the words, who allow the expressed feelings to fill us with the wonder of God's goodness. It is not much — but it must serve. It is all there is, so it is to this measure of חַיִּים that we cling.

※ ※ ※

We are now ready to move on to an analysis of the . . . וּכְתוֹב formula. We wondered why the wording is, . . . חַיִּים טוֹבִים and why there is reference to, בְּנֵי בְרִיתֶךָ.

What, exactly, is a בֶּן בְּרִית?

A בְּרִית is a *covenant*; the relationship which it establishes is one of mutual commitment and obligation. The partners enter into an association which imposes duties, demands compliance, assumes active and vital commitment and participation. A בֶּן בְּרִית is one who functions legitimately within such a framework.

How, if what Rav teaches is true, can we be בְּנֵי בְרִית of God? If our every instinct is ultimately inspired by God then what can we contribute? How are we equal partners with God?

Perhaps it is this conundrum which motivates us to ask for חַיִּים טוֹבִים in this context. During the *Aseres Yemei Teshuvah*, when the gates of heaven are so widely opened, we will not be satisfied with the low-grade חַיִּים of the ordinary. More and more we want to demonstrate our love by drawing upon our own resources. We will scale heights, plumb depths, breach barriers, discover greatness, achieve stature by bowing ever lower — will, in short, forge a *good life* out of *life*.

We will be proud partners in our covenant with God.

בְּסֵפֶר חַיִּים בְּרָכָה וְשָׁלוֹם . . .
In the Book Of Life Blessing and Peace and Good Livelihood . . .

In the final blessing of the *amidah* prayer we ask God for peace.[1]

Accordingly, we are not surprised that the fourth insertion asks God to remember us and to inscribes us, לְחַיִּים טוֹבִים וּלְשָׁלוֹם, for a good life *and for peace*. This even without having recourse to the suggestion made by *Rashi* [see previous essay] that our entreaties ought to move expansively from a request for simple חַיִּים [...זָכְרֵנוּ], through חַיִּים טוֹבִים [...וּכְתוֹב] to, טוֹבִים וּלְשָׁלוֹם in our blessing. The mention of שָׁלוֹם has a logic all of its own simply because *peace* is the focus of the host blessing.

But what of חַיִּים in this context. How does an entreaty for *life* fit into a blessing which has only *peace* on its agenda? Do *life* and *peace* form a cohesive unit? What precisely does the idea, חַיִּים טוֹבִים וְשָׁלוֹם convey?

---

1. The wording of the שִׂים שָׁלוֹם passage which we have in our *siddurim* appears to be an expansion of an earlier form which concentrated solely on the concept of שָׁלוֹם — as does the שָׁלוֹם רָב formula which, according to the Ashkenazi rite, we recite in our *minchah* and *maariv* prayers.

This suggestion is made by Eliezer Levi in his *Yesodos HaTefilah*. In support he cites a *Genizah* fragment which appears to date back to the Second Temple era and which reads: שִׂים שְׁלוֹמְךָ עַל יִשְׂרָאֵל עַמֶּךָ וְעַל עִירְךָ וְעַל נַחֲלָתְךָ וּבָרְכֵנוּ כּוּלָנוּ כְּאֶחָד. בָּרוּךְ אַתָּה ה׳ עוֹשֵׂה הַשָּׁלוֹם.

The additions — he feels — can be explained by a desire to echo the three ideas contained in the Kohanite blessings for which שִׂים שָׁלוֹם serves as a finale. Thus, . . . יְבָרֶכְךָ ה׳ is picked up by, שִׂים שָׁלוֹם טוֹבָה וּבְרָכָה. . . . יָאֵר ה׳ is paralleled by, . . . וְטוֹב בְּאוֹר פָּנֶיךָ. בָּרְכֵנוּ אָבִינוּ כּוּלָנוּ כְּאֶחָד בְּאוֹר פָּנֶיךָ. And וְיָשֵׂם לְךָ שָׁלוֹם . . . is echoed by, . . . בְּעֵינֶיךָ לְבָרֵךְ אֶת עַמְּךָ יִשְׂרָאֵל בְּכָל עֵת וּבְכָל שָׁעָה בִּשְׁלוֹמֶךָ.

In the previous essay we defined life as something that is independent and self-replenishing. Here we will take our analysis one stage further.

The way of life leads upwards for him who understands. This so that he may be saved from the nethermost depths (Proverbs 15:24). *Gra* remarks: Man is in a constant state of flux [הָאָדָם נִקְרָא הוֹלֵךְ ...]. He must always move from one level to the next — and if he does not move upwards he must God forbid, move downward, for it is impossible for him to stay in one place ...

Life, then, is to be equated with growth and development.

Thus, *Yoma* 71a on *Proverbs* 3:2, *for* [Torah and *Mitzvos*] *will grant you length of days and years of life* .... Are there years of living and years during which there is no life? R' Elazar taught: These [*years of living*] are such that he experiences a change from bad to good.

Apparently, then, an existence which is static, bereft of growth and development, is no life at all.

It is thus that commentators understand *Proverbs* 6:23: *For commands may be a lamp, Torah a light — but the path to life is made up of stern commitment to self-improvement* [תּוֹכְחוֹת מוּסָר]. The sense is that Torah and *mitzvos* are guides to living — never life itself. Life is the battlefield where the foe is one's own intractable and stubborn nature. It calls for unremitting struggle — brooks no half measures. It is a refusal to remain the same, a determination never to bask in the glow of hard-won achievement. It insists that yesterday's laurels become today's goading thorns. It is made up of many defeats — softened only occasionally by modest victories. There are strayings and regressions — the ultimate goal remains ever elusive, ever beyond reach. There are gut-wrenching disappointments, dreadful intimations of failure — the successes always seeming smaller and less significant than the what-might-have-beens.

Life, *Proverbs* teaches, is never peaceful.

And yet, in this last of the four insertions, we ask God for חַיִּים זכרנו לחיים — *Remember Us for Life*

טוֹבִים וְשָׁלוֹם, *a good life lived in peace*! Is there not here a contradiction in terms?

Perhaps peace need not be as peaceful as, at first, we would assume.

Certainly there is a peace which derives from the absolute harmony in which disparate components interact with and complement one another. We think of a piece of music in which each note enriches and colors the other to produce the loveliness which so deeply touches our hearts. But, to remain with our musical metaphor, discord and dissonance also have their place. They too, by providing contrast and piquancy, make their contribution. *Metzudos* to *Chronicles* notes that the very word which, in Hebrew, describes music, נִצּוּחַ, connotes *victory*, *the ability to overcome*, because the beauty of music derives from many voices or instruments vying with one another in a battle for beauty.

This second form, this harmony which draws upon the disharmonious to enhance its attractiveness, needs the firm hand of the composer to assign form, location and degree. Uncontrolled, it is nothing but raucous cacophony plaguing the ear and offending the senses.

The peace that describes the harmony born of discord is an *imposed* peace. It is born of raw power which has the strength to wrest beauty out of ugliness, elegance out of the ungainly and misformed.

It is not remarkable that both the peace which is God's own purview and that which He grants to His people is associated with power. Of the first, Bildad sang: *Dominion and awe are His, He spreads peace in the heights that are His* [הַמְשֵׁל וָפַחַד עִמּוֹ עֹשֶׂה שָׁלוֹם בִּמְרוֹמָיו] (*Iyov* 25:2). The second, from *Psalms* 29:11: H*ASHEM gives power to His people*, H*ASHEM blesses His people with peace* [ה׳ עֹז לְעַמּוֹ יִתֵּן ה׳ יְבָרֵךְ אֶת עַמּוֹ בַשָּׁלוֹם].

Evidently in both cases the second form of peace of which we spoke above is envisioned. As God's rulership [הַמְשֵׁל = מֶמְשָׁלָה]

imposes ultimate harmony upon the raging, warring elements, so the *strength* which God gave His people helps them to find a greater peace in the very struggles which inform and give meaning to their lives.

It is this peace which we have in mind when we ask God to inscribe us, לְחַיִּים טוֹבִים וּלְשָׁלוֹם.

וּבְכֵן תֵּן פַּחְדְּךָ ה' אֱלֹ-הֵינוּ עַל כָּל מַעֲשֶׂיךָ...
Now This Being So, O HASHEM Our God Instill All Those Whom You Made With Your Awe...

Before we begin an analysis of this passage which according to most *minhagim* is recited as part of the third [*kedushah*] blessing on Rosh Hashanah and Yom Kippur[1] we must spend a few moments considering the wording of the blessing itself.

---

1. Most, but not all. Thus, for example, *R' Saadyah Gaon* does not have the passage at all, and *Rambam* in his *Seder HaTefillah LeChol Hashanah* writes that only some congregations had the custom to recite the passage on Yom Kippur.

We may surmise that the thinking of those congregations which limited the recital of this passage to Rosh Hashanah, may have been as follows:

The *mishnah* in *Rosh Hashanah* (4:5) records the opinion of R' Yochanan ben Nuri that *Malchios* are to be recited as part of the third [*kedushah*] blessing, rather than in the fourth [*kedushas hayom*] blessing as is our custom in accord with the opinion of the Rabbi Akiva in that *mishnah*. Now a number of thinkers have suggested that it is possible that ... וּבְכֵן תֵּן פַּחְדְּךָ and the subsequent paragraphs may have been the introduction to *Malchios* according to the rite propagated by R' Yochanan ben Nuri. Certainly, if we judge by its content, and particularly from its final paragraph, ... וְתִמְלֹךְ this appears to be a distinct possibility.

This would certainly explain the usage of those congregations which, as *Rambam* reports, did not make this insertion on Yom Kippur.

The explanation may also be much simpler. The passage may have nothing to do with R' Yochanan ben Nuri's opinion and still be an appropriate addition to the *kedushah* blessing. As *Daniel Goldschmidt* demonstrates from a number of examples, the concepts of *kedushah* and *malchus* frequently appear together [כִּי אֵ-ל מֶלֶךְ גָּדוֹל וְקָדוֹשׁ אָתָּה.. from our own blessing is just one example] and the addition, to the blessing of *kedushah*, of a *piyut* which expounds on this theme needs no defense. Those congregations which did not include the prayer on Yom Kippur may simply have felt that it is appropriate only to Rosh Hashanah because on Yom Kippur the concept of *Malchios* does not play the central role which it does on Rosh Hashanah.

This blessing developed in three different forms. There is אַתָּה
קָדוֹשׁ וְשִׁמְךָ קָדוֹשׁ ... which we use in our daily prayers. There is,
קָדוֹשׁ אַתָּה וְנוֹרָא שְׁמֶךָ ... which at one time or in some rites seems
to have been the regular form of the blessing [see *Sifrey*,
Devarim 33:2 and *Pirkei d'Rabbi Eliezer* 35] but which in our
usage is reserved for Rosh Hashanah and Yom Kippur as an
ending to the וּבְכֵן תֵּן פַּחְדְּךָ insertion. And there is, לְדוֹר וָדוֹר נַגִּיד
גָּדְלֶךָ ... which, in the Ashkenazi rite, we use only in conjunction
with the קְדוּשָׁה. [2]

This given, we note that both in the silent *amidah* and during
the *chazzan's* repetition, we sandwich the *piyut* between two of
the three possible readings of the blessing. In the silent *amidah*
we begin with ... אַתָּה קָדוֹשׁ, proceed with the *piyut* and end
with, ... קָדוֹשׁ אַתָּה, while in the *chazzan's* repetition we begin,
immediately after the קְדוּשָׁה with ... לְדוֹר וָדוֹר and, once more,
end with ... קָדוֹשׁ אַתָּה.

With *Daniel Goldschmidt* we assume that there were two
original usages. One which had the *piyut* follow the blessing —
thus, for example in the *Siddur HaRambam* which has the
introductory ... אַתָּה קָדוֹשׁ but omits the concluding ... קָדוֹשׁ אַתָּה
— and one which had the *piyut* precede the blessing.

---

2. The following may be the logic by which we substitute ... לְדוֹר וָדוֹר for the
regular wording when the קְדוּשָׁה is recited.

The regular wording, according to our usage, is made up of two concepts:
אַתָּה קָדוֹשׁ וְשִׁמְךָ קָדוֹשׁ which is a proclamation of God's sanctity; and וּקְדוֹשִׁים בְּכָל
יוֹם יְהַלְלוּךָ ... which asserts that Israel [the קְדוֹשִׁים of this phrase according to
many commentators] praises God every day.

Now the ... לְדוֹר וָדוֹר passage speaks only of this second element. It does not
affirm God's sanctity but tells of our determination to constantly sing God's
praises.

It may well be that this was seen as a fitting ending for the קְדוּשָׁה which,
itself, takes the place of the first part of the normal blessing. Certainly
the proclamation, ... קָדוֹשׁ קָדוֹשׁ קָדוֹשׁ ה' צְבָ-אוֹת is a natural stand-in for, אַתָּה
קָדוֹשׁ ...

If this theory is correct, then the custom of saying ... לְדוֹר וָדוֹר would serve
as a strong proof for those who claim that קְדוֹשִׁים in the phrase, וּקְדוֹשִׁים בְּכָל יוֹם
... refers to Israel rather than, as some commentators contend, to the angels.

Our usage would then be a combination of the two customs.

Now it is a truism that in attempting to interpret our prayers, we ought to ignore historical development and, instead, to deal with the forms which have come down to us. For our purposes this would mean that we are justified in interpreting the *piyut* as we have it, sandwiched, as it were, between an introductory אַתָּה קָדוֹשׁ ... and a concluding ... קָדוֹשׁ אַתָּה, without reference to the fact that, in its original incarnation it would not have carried the same nuances.

With this assumption in place we shall now address ourselves to an examination of the *piyut* as it speaks to us in its present form. We have made a point of stressing that the קְדוֹשִׁים in the phrase, ... וּקְדוֹשִׁים בְּכָל יוֹם ... refers to Israel and not, as some commentators maintain, to the angels. This given, let us examine the function of this phrase.

One implication seems clear: the statement, *You are holy and Your name is holy* cannot stand on its own. It somehow lacks body and content unless there are *holy ones* who sing His praises.

We understand this as follows: Sanctity is an idea which makes sense only in a relative context. One cannot be holy except in relation to that which is profane. Moreover, if the two domains, the sacred and the profane, are to exist meaningfully there must be someone who apprehends the contrast between them. Absent such awareness the state of being holy is denuded of any content.

Hence the trilogy: *You are holy; Your name is holy; holy ones sing Your praises.* If we postulate, as in this context we may, that *name* is that aspect of the Divine to which man can relate, then it is the bridge which connects the otherwise inaccessible *You* with the *holy ones* who must be brought into the picture if the statement *You are holy* is to make sense.

We feel convinced that the continuum: *You are holy ... and holy ones* [read, Israel] *sing Your praises* is based on the verse in

וְאַתָּה קָדוֹשׁ יוֹשֵׁב תְּהִלּוֹת יִשְׂרָאֵל, *Psalms*, *You are holy waiting expectantly [thus the midrash to* יוֹשֵׁב*] for Israel's praises* (*Psalms* 22:4). If God *waits expectantly* for Israel's praises that can only mean that, without them, there can be no meaning to אַתָּה קָדוֹשׁ, *You are holy*.

But, if we are correct in this assumption, why change the *Israel* of the *Psalms* verse to *kedoshim*. Why not, ... *and Israel sings Your praises every day*?

Perhaps the change is rooted in the uniqueness of Jewish prayer.

Prayer is not the exclusive preserve of the Jewish people; *For My house shall be proclaimed as a house of prayer for all the people* (*Isaiah* 56:7). But, having said that, there is still a vast difference between our prayer and that of the nations. It is only we who are God's children and have the right to approach Him as *father*, only we who are His special servants and thus can lay our entire individual and national being at His feet. The insistence that our *amidah* grow out of our perception of ourselves as a nation redeemed סְמִיכוּת גְּאוּלָה לִתְפִלָּה; the *Avos* blessing with which we introduce ourselves to God, both derive from this singularity.

All people pray; Israel prays differently.

And that is because we are holy.

Who we are; what our history has made of us and what we have made of ourselves; the *Avos* who stand behind us, the messianic future which beckons through the haze of the unknown; our struggles and our hopes; the hatred which we inspire and the love of which we are capable; our homecomings and our exiles; our vulnerability and our indestructibility — all these and the myriad other details which make up the impenetrable maze of our history, have hammered us into a people which is no stranger to holiness. We may be hardput to define it, are acutely aware that often our actions and our thoughts are not in consonance with its expectations and demands, but we know — know with absolute certainty — that it defines our being.

And as a Holy People we sing God's praises.

The third blessing — in its וְאַתָּה קָדוֹשׁ incarnation — talks of Israel as much as it talks of God. God is holy. But Israel — more than any nation — understands this holiness.

❧ ❧ ❧

This analysis of the third blessing as it has come to us in our rite can now serve as background to the וּבְכֵן תֵּן פַּחְדְּךָ insertion. Once more we stress that the relationship between the two is not absolute. That is, we must recognize that quite possibly the *piyut* may at one time have been said with the קָדוֹשׁ אַתָּה version of the third blessing which, at least in the form in which it has come down to us, says nothing at all about Israel's uniqueness. In such a context it would not carry the precise nuances which we can readily detect in its present incarnation. Nevertheless we feel it important to interpret the passage as it now stands because that is the reality with which we have to deal.

Let us then read the *piyut* as a celebration of the uniqueness of Israel, the קְדוֹשִׁים who alone are able to really sing the praises of HASHEM.

The passage lends itself readily to such an interpretation because there is a discernible narrowing of its focus. It begins with כָּל מַעֲשֶׂיךָ, *All those whom You have created*; continues with, עַמֶּךָ, *Your people*; and then goes to צַדִּיקִים , *the righteous* among them. Clearly such a system is designed to stress the special and particular status of each of the more and more focused sub-groups.

If then כָּל מַעֲשֶׂיךָ is a term which includes all of mankind, then the second paragraph, . . . וּבְכֵן תֵּן כָּבוֹד is designed to show how *Your people* in particular is deserving of the *kavod* of which the passage speaks.

We have noted that the first paragraph talks of כָּל מַעֲשֶׂיךָ while the second focuses upon עַמֶּךָ. A careful reading yields other differences. The spirit which pervades the first is one of fear, we speak of פַּחַד, אֵימָה and יִרְאָה, while the second one is suffused with joy — the operative terms are, שִׂמְחָה, תִּקְוָה טוֹבָה, כָּבוֹד and שָׂשׂוֹן.

Herewith the *Midrash Tanchuma's* (end of *Noach*) depiction of the respective roles which the nations and Israel will play in the End of Days.

There is a Messianic future for the nations of the world as much as there is for Israel. History is nothing if not an inexorable — if agonizingly slow — progression towards a truth which the whole of mankind will, in the end, be bound to apprehend. No one — with the one exception of incorrigible Amalek — will be excluded. Nevertheless the slate of accumulated historical guilt will not be wiped entirely clean. The burden of shame with which the nations in their perfidy have loaded themselves will not be dissipated. They will be welcomed only as servants doing a master's bidding, will have to be constantly fearful of making a mistake which — in the nature of the master-servant relationship — will not easily be forgiven. Their relationship to God will be one of trembling and insecurity. They share in the Messianic idyll — but only just.

By contrast, Israel will be, as they have always been, God's beloved children. No recriminations — even if, as children they occasionally fall short of their filial obligations — will becloud the unconditional love with which God favors them. The bonds forged in the searing flames of their dreadful history can withstand the inevitable disappointments which must be a part of even the most perfect relationship. The mood is one of security and happiness. Israel will experience the Messianic bliss as it should be savored.

This is the *kavod* of which our passage speaks. כָּבוֹד a derivative of כָּבֵד, *to be heavy*, is neither intrinsic nor absolute.

Just as weight has significance only for the person who stands outside the object and must grapple with its intractability, so too is כָּבוֹד a function of the beholder's perceptions. The sense of the *kavod* for which we beg God is that the nations may finally come to recognize Israel's unique affinity to the holiness which, although throughout the ages it remained unperceived and unrespected, was always the key to the riddle of their exile existence.

In this sense the first section, [וּבְכֵן תֵּן פַּחְדְּךָ] is a necessary and indispensable precondition to the second. Only once the nations will — with awe and trembling — have shouldered their historic role of forming one association with only the fulfillment of God's will as its charter [וְיֵעָשׂוּ כוּלָם אֲגוּדָה אַחַת לַעֲשׂוֹת רְצוֹנְךָ בְּלֵבָב שָׁלֵם], will they be psychologically able to render us that honor which is the mark of our uniqueness.

Once we have attained the *honor* which is our due, we have an agenda of our own. We want, first and foremost, the opportunity to do that which we do best, and which, if our interpretation of וּקְדוֹשִׁים בְּכָל יוֹם יְהַלְלוּךָ . . . is correct, is the focal point of the entire sequence with which we are dealing: We beg that God grant us, who stand in awe of him, תְּהִלָּה — such experiences as will stimulate us to praise Him. For that, as the commentators make clear, is the meaning of this phrase. It harks back to the beginning of the blessing. God, as we saw above, *waits expectantly* for Israel's praises [תְּהִלּוֹת יִשְׂרָאֵל]. Our prayer is that we might be given the opportunity to do that which is expected of us.

Why good hope to *those who seek You out*, תִּקְוָה טוֹבָה לְדוֹרְשֶׁיךָ, in this context?

Because Israel's praises express themselves most authentically in Israel's longings, The servant's task, difficult as it may be, may at some point be completed; the goad of love which leaves the son no rest, drives ever onwards. We are to be perpetual seekers, and as seekers — hopers. When Noach's [gentile] son Shem sought a name for the future Jerusalem he called it *Shalem*, the place in which absolute fulfillment can be attained. The concept of being finally done, of everything being in place with nothing at all left to be accomplished [שָׁלֵם], had its place in his religious philosophy.

Our father Abraham had a different vision. ה׳ יִרְאֶה, *Hashem will yet see*. He perceived the *Akeidah* — surely, we might have thought, the ultimate in challenges beyond which nothing more ought to be expected — as a beginning, not an end. There will, he knew and hoped, be other muscles to be flexed, other, as yet unsuspected horizons to tantalize and beckon.

What are we to make of פִּתְחוֹן פֶּה לַמְיַחֲלִים לָךְ?

The term occurs in *Ezekiel* 29:21 where, as *Rashi* understands it, it appears to have the meaning, *vindication*. After certain events were to come about, everyone would realize that, all along, Yechezkel's prophecies had been correct. This would give him, a פִּתְחוֹן פֶּה — presumably in relation to those people who had earlier denied the validity of his predictions. He would be vindicated. Apparently, then, the words are to be rendered idiomatically and it is thus that it should probably be understood in Rabbinic usage such as, ... שֶׁלֹּא לִיתֵּן פִּתְחוֹן פֶּה לְמִינִים.

Thus, for our phrase: *Grant vindication to those who pin their hopes upon You.*

The sense in our context would be as follows. Before the Messianic era, trust in God often appears to remain unrequited. With maddening perversity the purest and holiest among us are often exposed to the most dreadful of fates. Longing appears to invite rejection, warm hope rams up against a wall of what sometimes appears to be icy indifference.

The haunting riddle of the suffering of the righteous has, since time immemorial, provided an unsettling background to the struggles of believers who had to remain undaunted by a reality which more often than not seemed to scoff their faith. Every explanation seemed only to raise more questions, every justification was either superfluous for the stubborn saint, or unconvincing to even those questioners who would gladly have been persuaded.

It is not easy to be a believer in a world which has distanced itself from God's loving embrace.

But — the time will come when it will become clear that God is the Holy One Who *waits expectantly* for Israel's praise. Israel's longing for God will be seen to have been no more than the mirror image of, as it were, God's longing for Israel. The questions which plagued us in the past will find their answers or, better still, will in the ecstasy of rediscovered love, cease altogether to matter.

Those that pinned their hope upon God will have found vindication.

And, once more the land will rejoice; once more God's city will be glad [שִׂמְחָה לְאַרְצֶךָ וְשָׂשׂוֹן לְעִירֶךָ].

How are we to understand the juxtaposition of land to people? Why is there a natural flow from Israel's vindication to the land's delight?

It derives from a symbiotic relationship which lies at the very crux of Jewish experience.

And I shall lay the Land waste, and your enemies which seek to dwell upon it will experience its wastedness! (Leviticus 26:32).

The *Tochachah* in *Bechukosai* spells out in graphic and shocking detail the terrible exile experience which will come about when we will have failed to live up to the Torah's demands for a holy people in a holy land. We hear of Israel bewildered and disoriented, away from the familiar ambience of its beloved home, of the alien cultures which will suck us up in their greedy maws, of the terrors which will grind away at our self-confidence to a point at which the sound of a rustling leaf will drive us into panicky flight.

All this we expect. If the threat of impending exile is to help us avoid sin, then we must know, and if possible see in our mind's eye, the full range of its horrors.

But there is another motif — tones, scattered throughout this threnody of despair, which portend a glimmer of hope. Again and again we are shown a land uncultivated and unyielding, of ruined cities stubbornly clinging to their emptiness — of *Eretz Yisrael* pining for its children.

This is what *Ramban* has to say:

> ... [The statement that our] enemies would experience its wastedness, is a message of hope. It affirms that throughout our exiles, our land would never welcome our enemies.
>
> This serves as powerful proof and potent promise! For nowhere else will you find a land which had always been fertile and generous, always full of people, which is now as devastated as is [Eretz Yisrael].
>
> For from the moment that we left it, it refused to accept any other people. All attempted to settle it — none succeeded.

As the *paytan* looks into the future, he sees not only a proud, self-conscious and self-confident people, but also a renewed and rejoicing land.

❈ ❈ ❈

The *piyut* now takes an unexpected turn. The sharpening of focus from *all Your creations* to, *Your people* was natural within the structure which we have discovered, and therefore expected. Israel is vindicated as those ideally suited to sing God's praises. But what is the logic of isolating the *righteous*, the *upright* and the *pious* within the nation? Certainly those who have wrested these distinctions from the sea of mediocrity within which most of us flounder are worthy of admiration. They lend luster to our peoplehood and we bask in the reflected glory of their attainments. But why is this the context within which to mark their singularity?

Let us examine more closely the standing of the *tzaddik* within our nation.

The second part of our paragraph is particularly revealing: ... *Iniquity will clamp its mouth, all wickedness will dissipate like smoke — when the reign of evil will have passed from the land.*

What exactly is this *reign of evil*? Why is its passing tied to the rejoicing of the righteous among us?

When our Sages teach that it is only the *talmidei chachamim* among us who can truly be described as kings [רבנן איקרי מלכים (*Gittin* 62a)] they are not indulging in hyperbole. People need inspiration, they look to men who, in their persons and by their actions, define, refine and exemplify national ideals and aspirations. Let the political structure of a given society be what it may, there will always be followers and those whose charisma and abilities mark them as leaders.[3]

And so, there is always the question of who, in any given grouping, will assume the royal mantle. Certainly, absolutes are rare and a nuanced stance the norm. But in its essential elements the choice is clear-cut and unambiguous. The ruler will exert either a benign or a malignant influence. He will personify the *reign of evil* or be the *talmid chacham*-king of whom the Sages spoke.

We said before that the great among us lend luster to our society. They do more. They define its nature, give Jewish peoplehood its body and direction. We wondered why the *piyut* moves from the singularity of *Your nation* to the celebration of the righteous among them. The answer has become clear: *Your nation* remains an amorphous and murky concept unless the righteous within it rejoice, the upright jubilate and the pious celebrate with song.

With Israel's authentic leadership in place, iniquity dissipates and the *reign of evil* disappears from the land.

❦ ❦ ❦

---

3. It is worthy of note that the root [מלך] from which the noun, [מֶלֶךְ], *king*, is formed, has the meaning, *to rule*, in its active form, but, *to seek advice or guidance* in the *nif'al*, passive. Apparently a king is one to whom the people look for inspiration.

The *piyut* now moves on to a truth beneath the truth: When the righteous, the upright and the pious stand at the helm of the ship of state, it is in reality God Who, in His awesome majesty, is the true, the only King. The righteous are no more than the conduit through which His will becomes manifest. Mount Zion and Jerusalem are the locus of a Divine stewardship of human affairs which remains ultimately unencumbered and unobscured by any human involvement.

וְתִמְלֹךְ אַתָּה ה׳ לְבַדֶּךָ, *You, O God will reign alone!*

❈ ❈ ❈

With this, the *piyut* comes to a close.

We must now find room in our scheme for the ... קָדוֹשׁ אַתָּה reading of the third blessing which rounds off the passage. We noted above that our custom of, as it were, sandwiching the *piyut* between two different versions of the קְדוּשָׁה blessing probably derives from the combination of two discrete rites one of which had it precede the *piyut*, the other, to follow it. What, in our version, does this second reading of the blessing add to what has already been said?

Perhaps the answer lies in the omission of any mention of Israel as the ideal singers of God's praises in this version. The assertion that, ... קְדוֹשִׁים בְּכָל יוֹם יְהַלְלוּךָ had its legitimate place in our contemplation of God's sanctity. But not any more. After we have come to the recognition that God alone must be the ruler of ideal Israel in the Messianic future [... וְתִמְלֹךְ אַתָּה ה׳ לְבַדֶּךָ] we want to focus exclusively upon Him. It is His awesome sanctity, not our ability to have some grasp of it, which grips our mind.

אֱלֹהֵינוּ וֵאלֹהֵי אֲבוֹתֵינוּ 🙥
מְלוֹךְ עַל כָּל הָעוֹלָם כֻּלּוֹ בִּכְבוֹדֶךָ . . .
Our God and the God of Our Forefathers, Reign Over the Entire Universe in Your Glory . . .

The *tefilos* of Sabbath and *Yom Tov* [with the exception of *mussaf* on Rosh Hashanah which has three] allow for just one blessing between the opening and concluding sets of three. This blessing is known as *kedushas hayom* — it celebrates the *sanctity* of each of these holy days. *Rosh Chodesh* too has its *kedushas hayom*, but it is said only during *mussaf*.

The words with which we have entitled this essay introduce the concluding section of the *kedushas hayom* blessing of Rosh Hashanah.

We can best appreciate the profound significance of the wording in this passage by comparing it with the parallel section of the other *kedushas hayom* blessings.

Sabbath:

אֱלֹהֵינוּ וֵאלֹהֵי אֲבוֹתֵינוּ רְצֵה בִמְנוּחָתֵנוּ . . ., *Our God and the God of our forefathers, may You be pleased with our rest . . . .*

Yom Tov [Non-*musaf*]:

וְהַשִּׂיאֵנוּ ה׳ אֱלֹהֵינוּ אֶת בִּרְכַּת מוֹעֲדֶיךָ . . ., *Bestow upon us O HASHEM, our God, the blessing of your appointed Festivals . . . .*

Yom Tov [*musaf*]:

אֱלֹהֵינוּ וֵאלֹהֵי אֲבוֹתֵינוּ מֶלֶךְ רַחֲמָן רַחֵם עָלֵינוּ . . . בְּנֵה בֵיתְךָ כְּבַתְּחִלָּה . . ., *Our God and the God of our forefathers, O* merciful King have mercy on us; . . . . Rebuild Your House as it was at first . . . .

Rosh Chodesh:

אֱלֹ־הֵינוּ וֵאלֹ־הֵי אֲבוֹתֵינוּ חַדֵּשׁ עָלֵינוּ אֶת הַחֹדֶשׁ הַזֶּה לְטוֹבָה וְלִבְרָכָה . . ., *Our God and the God of our forefathers, inaugurate for us this month for good and for blessing . . . .*

Rosh Hashanah:

אֱלֹ־הֵינוּ וֵאלֹ־הֵי אֲבוֹתֵינוּ מְלוֹךְ עַל כָּל הָעוֹלָם כֻּלּוֹ בִּכְבוֹדֶךָ . . ., *Our God and the God of our forefathers reign over the entire universe in Your glory . . . .*

Yom Kippur:

אֱלֹ־הֵינוּ וֵאלֹ־הֵי אֲבוֹתֵינוּ מְחַל לַעֲווֹנוֹתֵינוּ בְּיוֹם הַכִּפֻּרִים הַזֶּה . . ., *Our God and the God of our forefathers, forgive our sins on this Yom Kippur . . . .*

The wording which we use on Sabbath, *Yom Tov* and *Rosh Chodesh* is precisely as we would have expected it to be. We address ourselves to those aspects of these days which lend them their unique character and thereby we solemnize and affirm their sanctity.

The Yom Kippur text, in that it asks God to forgive our sins, seems to veer from this usage — but it is not a radical departure. The atoning function of Yom Kippur is vested in the nature of the day itself [. . . וְעַצְמוֹ שֶׁל יוֹם מְכַפֵּר לַשָּׁבִים, *the very day [by its nature] atones for those who repent. . .* (Rambam, *Hilchos Teshuvah* 1:3)] and a petition for absolution can thus be viewed as testament to the day's sanctity.

The Rosh Hashanah wording is more problematic. To understand the difficulty and to find our way towards a solution we must subject *Rosh Hashanah* 32a to closer analysis.

❧ ❧ ❧

The Gemara's discussion revolves around the verse in *Leviticus* 23:24 which reads as follows: . . . בַּחֹדֶשׁ הַשְּׁבִיעִי בְּאֶחָד לַחֹדֶשׁ יִהְיֶה

לָכֶם שַׁבָּתוֹן זִכְרוֹן תְּרוּעָה מִקְרָא קֹדֶשׁ. The four expressions, שַׁבָּתוֹן, זִכְרוֹן, תְּרוּעָה and מִקְרָא קֹדֶשׁ are all presumed to hint at specific *halachos* and the Gemara reports a disagreement about how best to utilize them.

From where, the Gemara asks, do we know that on Rosh Hashanah we are to say *Malchios*, *Zichronos* and *Shoforos*? Two opinions are offered:

R' Elazar:

שַׁבָּתוֹן: Teaches that we are to recite the blessing of *kedushas hayom*.

זִכְרוֹן: Teaches that we are to say *Zichronos*.

תְּרוּעָה: Teaches that we are to say *Shoforos*.

מִקְרָא קֹדֶשׁ: Teaches that certain labors are forbidden to us on Rosh Hashanah.

R' Akiva:

שַׁבָּתוֹן: Teaches that certain labors are forbidden to us on Rosh Hashanah.

זִכְרוֹן: Teaches that we are to say *Zichronos*.

תְּרוּעָה: Teaches that we are to say *Shoforos*.

מִקְרָא קֹדֶשׁ: Teaches that we are to recite the blessing of *kedushas hayom*.

At this point we still do not have a source for the recitation of *Malchios*.

For this the Gemara quotes two opinions:

Rebbi suggests the following: Immediately before the *Yom Tov* of Rosh Hashanah is introduced, at *Leviticus* 23:23, the Torah deals with the obligation to leave פֵּאָה, *a portion of the harvest*, for the poor. The sentence which tells us of this *mitzvah* ends with the words, אֲנִי ה' אֱל-הֵיכֶם ..., *I am* HASHEM *your God*. This phrase can be viewed as a springboard from which the *Yom Tov* of Rosh Hashanah is introduced [אֲנִי ה' ... אֱל־הֵיכֶם ... וּבַחֹדֶשׁ הַשְּׁבִיעִי ...]. It, as it were, flows from the proposition that God is our Lord — itself the concept of *Malchios*.

Rabbi Yose ben Yehudah goes to *Numbers* 10:1-10 where we learn of the trumpets which Moses was commanded to fashion for himself. V.10, there, reads as follows: וּבְיוֹם שִׂמְחַתְכֶם וּבְמוֹעֲדֵיכֶם וּבְרָאשֵׁי חָדְשֵׁכֶם וּתְקַעְתֶּם בַּחֲצֹצְרוֹת עַל עֹלֹתֵיכֶם וְעַל זִבְחֵי שַׁלְמֵיכֶם וְהָיוּ לָכֶם לְזִכָּרוֹן לִפְנֵי אֱל־הֵיכֶם אֲנִי ה' אֱל־הֵיכֶם. *Now on the days of your rejoicing and on your appointed days and on your new-moon celeb*rations *you shall blow trumpets as you offer up your burnt offerings and your peace offerings. They shall serve as a memorial for you before your God. I am* HASHEM, *your God.*

The Gemara is troubled by the final phrase. How does, *I am* HASHEM *your God* augment what was said before? The solution is offered that the phrase is included here in order to produce a juxtaposition between, אֲנִי ה' אֱל־הֵיכֶם [*Malchios*] and, וְהָיוּ לָכֶם לְזִכָּרוֹן [*Zichronos*]. Just as here, *Malchios* follows hard upon *Zichronos*, so too, whenever *Zichronos* are required they are to be accompanied by *Malchios*. [זֶה בָּנָה אָב לְכָל מָקוֹם שֶׁנֶּאֱמַר בּוֹ זִכְרוֹנוֹת יִהְיוּ מַלְכִיּוֹת עִמָּהֶן] (*Rosh Hashanah*).

What does, לכל מקום, *wherever*, imply. Where, besides on Rosh Hashanah, does this rule have application?

The *mishnah* in *Taanis* 15a teaches that when, because of threatening droughts, a series of fast-days were imposed upon the community, the regular *amidah* prayer was expanded from its normal eighteen blessings to twenty-four. Two of the additional six blessings were, in the opinion of the *tana kama*, to be the same *Zichronos* and *Shoforos* which are normally said on Rosh Hashanah. R' Yehudah disagrees, for, *Zichronos* and *Shoforos* were only to be said on Rosh Hashanah, *Yovel* and in time of war (16b and 17a, there).

Both the opinion of the *tana kama* that *Zichronos* and *Shoforos* [but not *Malchios*] are to be recited on a *taanis*, and R' Yehudah's assertion that these are reserved for Rosh Hashanah, *Yovel* and time of war need to be examined in the light of the Gemara in *Rosh Hashanah* which we have just learned.

Tosafos Yom Tov to *Taanis* asks how the opinion of the *tana kama* that only *Zichronos* and *Shoforos* are to be recited can be reconciled with the rule enunciated in *Rosh Hashanah* that whenever *Zichronos* are required they are to be accompanied by *Malchios*. In the context of our discussion we do well in accepting the solution which *Meromei Sadeh* [*Netziv*] offers. He feels that the expression which *Rosh Hashanah* uses: ... כָּל מָקוֹם שֶׁנֶּאֱמַר בָּהּ זִכְרוֹנוֹת, implies that the rule is binding only on such instances where the requirement to recite *Zichronos* is somehow grounded in Scriptural text. The recitation of *Zichronos* and *Shoforos* on a communal fast-day has absolutely no Scriptural basis and derives solely from a Rabbinical ordinance and therefore it does not fall within the rubric of *Rosh Hashanah*'s ruling.

Thus equipped, we are ready to deal with R' Yehudah's assertion that the recitation of *Zichronos* and *Shoforos* is limited to, Rosh Hashanah, *Yovel* and times of war.

Let us examine each of these instances separately.

Rosh Hashanah is simple enough and the recitation of *Malchios* in addition to *Zichronos* and *Shoforos* can be justified on the basis of *Netziv*'s idea. Certainly there is a Scriptural basis to the recitation of *Zichronos* on Rosh Hashanah [see the Gemara paraphrased within] and thus the rule that, *whenever* Zichronos are required they are to be accompanied by *Malchios* is germane.

The case of *Yovel* is less simple. The source for the obligation to recite *Malchios*, *Zichronos* and *Shoforos* on the Yom Kipur of *Yovel* which is its Rosh Hashanah, derives from the *mishnah*, *Rosh Hashanah* 26b: [Yom Kippur of] *Yovel* is identical to Rosh Hashanah in regard to the obligation to sound [the shofar] and that the blessings [of *Malchios*, *Zichronos* and *Shoforos*] are to be said.

To this *Rashi* remarks: Although the shofar [of the *Yovel*] is neither a part of a prayer service nor does it have the function of generating rememberance [וְלֹא לְזִכָּרוֹן], but is nothing more than an indication that slaves are to be freed and fields returned to their original owners — still it is to be done just as on Rosh Hashanah because the laws of *Yovel* are compared to those of Rosh Hashanah based on a *gezeira shava* ...

As *Rashi* makes clear, there is no *rememberance* function to the shofar blasts of the *Yovel*. By the same token we must assume that the *Zichronos* which are to be recited do not inhere in the nature of the *Yovel* but derive from the same *gezeira shava* to which *Rashi* makes reference. Thus we conclude that the obligation to recite *Malchios*, *Zichronos* and *Shoforos* on the Yom Kippur of *Yovel* is taken in its entirety from the comparison to Rosh Hashanah and therefore ought not to be seen as an application of the rule that *Malchios* are to be recited whenever *Zichronos* are required.

This leaves us with the third category: *Time of war*. *Rashi* explains that the Gemara's assumption that *Zichronos* and *Shoforos* are to be recited in time of war is based upon *Numbers* 10:9: *Now when you shall come to war in your land against an oppressor who oppresses you, then you shall blow a teruah on trumpets and thus be remembered before HASHEM your God and saved from your enemies.*

Rashi continues: We are not aware of any source which requires that the verses of *Malchios*, *Zichronos* and *Shoforos* be recited in time of war.

The commentators wonder why *Rashi* mentions *Malchios* in this context. The Gemara is discussing only *Zichronos* and *Shoforos*. Various explanations are offered and any of them may well justify *Rashi's* assumption. For our purpose it is sufficient to note that *Rashi* does, unequivocally, state that *Malchios* are to be recited in times of war. This could well be explained by the suggestion of *Meromei Sadeh* which we quoted above. The rule laid down in *Rosh Hashanah* is that *Malchios* are to be recited whenever *Zichronos* are required — and where that requirement has its source in the Scriptural text. Since the *Zichronos* which are to be recited in time of war are in fact hinted at in the verse quoted by *Rashi*, the conclusion that *Malchios* should also be said is inevitable.

We began this discussion with the question of what areas might be covered by the expression, לכל מקום. Our analysis has yielded the exclusion of *taanis* and *Yovel*, but the inclusion of Rosh Hashanah and *time of war*.

Significantly, both opinions agree that the source for *Malchios* lies outside the *parashah* of Rosh Hashanah. Within the *parasha* only the obligation to recite *Zichronos* and *Shoforos* is explicated. *Malchios* is either relegated to the *parashah* of *pe'ah* and applied to Rosh Hashanah only because of the proximity of the two *parshios*, or it is presented as being subsidiary to *Zichronos*: We say it only because of the rule that, ... *whenever Zichronos are required they are to be accompanied by Malchios*.

Now the requirement that a blessing of *kedushas hayom* be recited on Rosh Hashanah does have a basis within the *parashah* of Rosh Hashanah. We recall that it is derived either from the expression, שַׁבָּתוֹן or from מִקְרָא קֹדֶשׁ.[1]

Logic would therefore seem to demand that the content of the *kedushas hayom* blessing on Rosh Hashanah should be independent of the concept of *Malchios*. The wording of the passage which we placed at the beginning of this essay clearly puts paid to this argument. *Malchios* appears to be firmly entrenched in the *kedushas hayom* of Rosh Hashanah.

---

1. As we saw at the beginning of this essay, the *kedushas hayom* blessing is not unique to Rosh Hashanah, but is recited also on the Sabbath and on all the holidays.

Rashi to *Leviticus* 23:35 derives this obligation from the expression מִקְרָא קֹדֶשׁ. He makes his remarks to that term as it appears in connection with Yom Kippur: ... Affirm its sanctity by wearing clean clothes and through prayer [on Yom Kippur]. On the other holydays — with food, drink, clean clothes and prayer. [Rabbi Ch. D. Chavel adduces *Toras Kohanim* as *Rashi's* source but notes that *Toras Kohanim* does not have, ובתפלה.]

Ramban, too, appears to accept *Rashi's* interpretation. He derives the term מִקְרָא from קרא, *to summon* and explains מִקְרָאֵי קֹדֶשׁ: ... That on this day all are summoned and gathered together to make it holy. For it is a *mitzvah* for all Israel to gather in the Temple on an appointed day to celebrate its sanctity in public with *prayer* and praises to God and with clean clothes and to make it a day of feasting.

However this interpretation of מִקְרָא קֹדֶשׁ is not universally accepted. *Shevuos* 13a talks of one who did not imbue Yom Kippur with the status of מִקְרָא קֹדֶשׁ. *Rashi*, consistent with his commentary to *Chumash*, explains that this is one who did not recite the blessing of *kedushas hayom*. *Tosafos* however rejects this interpretation. The recitation of the blessing of *kedushas hayom* is of Rabbinic origin and consequently it cannot be said to reside in the meaning of the Torah's phrase, מִקְרָא קֹדֶשׁ.

Both the opinion of *Rashi* and that of *Tosaphos* call for closer analysis which lies beyond the scope of this essay. *Rashi's* view that the source for the *kedushas hayom* blessing is to be sought in the meaning of מִקְרָא קֹדֶשׁ does not allow for the *kedushas hayom* blessing of *Rosh Chodesh* — which is never associated with that term. *Tosafos* which does not trace the blessing to the expression and must therefore assume that it was ordained independently of any Scriptural reference will need to explain why, as we have seen in the passage which we have paraphrased within, the *kedushas hayom* blessing of Rosh Hashanah is based on one or the other of the words assigned to it by Rebbi and R' Yose ben Yehudah respectively.

❦ ❦ ❦

We need to examine the concept of *Malchios* more closely. What precisely is implied by proclaiming God as *king* on Rosh Hashanah?

We take note that according to both opinions, that of Rebbi and that of R' Yose ben Yehudah, the obligation to recite *Malchios* derives from a phrase in which the word מֶלֶךְ does not appear. Apparently אֲנִי ה׳ אֱלֹ-הֵיכֶם encapsulates the idea of מַלְכוּת as clearly as though the actual term had been used.[2]

Now the use of the combination of ה׳ and אֱלֹ-הִים to denote kingship is well established throughout the Torah. Thus the שְׁמַע, the verse most closely associated with the concept of, קַבָּלַת עוֹל מַלְכוּת שָׁמַיִם, *the shouldering of the yoke of heavenly kingship*,

---

2. The more so our surprise that this phrase seems not to qualify for inclusion among the verses which comprise the body of the *Malchios*. This transpires clearly from *Rosh Hashanah* 32b which states that in the whole Torah there are only three verses in which we talk of God as king. Of all other references to God, only . . . שְׁמַע יִשְׂרָאֵל is deemed as implying kingship within the sense of the *halachic* requirements for *Malchios*.

How is it possible that the very phrase which teaches that we are obligated to recite *Malchios* cannot be recited as affirming that concept?

We may surmise as follows: *Numbers* 15:41 reads: אֲנִי ה׳ אֱלֹ-הֵיכֶם אֲשֶׁר הוֹצֵאתִי אֶתְכֶם מֵאֶרֶץ מִצְרָיִם . . . אֲנִי ה׳ אֱלֹ-הֵיכֶם. The phrase אֲנִי ה׳ אֱלֹ-הֵיכֶם is repeated. To the first phrase *Rashi* remarks as expected: I can be relied upon to reward. To the second he says: Why is this repeated? So that Israel should not say, "Why has God told us [to serve Him]? Is it not that we should serve Him and thus earn reward? We will forgo the reward and not serve!" I am your king whether you want it or not!

Apparently the phrase on its own conveys only a partial picture. It does indeed hint at God as One Who rewards and punishes — a function which as we work out below, within, is rooted in kingship. But that, since it leaves room for people to say that they are willing to go without the rewards or to suffer the punishments, is not the whole picture. To convey the absoluteness of God's kingship the phrase had to be repeated.

Accordingly we understand well why the phrase on its own does not qualify as *Malchios*. It projects an imperfect picture in a context in which more is required.

talks of God as, ה' אֱלֹ־הֵינוּ. So too, the Ten Commandments which, according to *Mechilta* to *Yisro* are to be understood as God's proclamation of His kingship [... אֶמְלֹךְ עֲלֵיכֶם] are introduced by the phrase, אָנֹכִי ה' אֱלֹ־הֶיךָ.

Nevertheless we should wonder why just this phrase rather than the actual word מֶלֶךְ is used to teach us the obligation of reciting *Malchios* on Rosh Hashanah, both according to Rebbi and according to R' Yose ben Yehudah. It is surely no coincidence that these *Tana'im* who disagree so profoundly concerning the source for the obligation nevertheless found the same phrase in use in both places.

We suspect that the reason may be as follows:

The phrase, אֲנִי ה' אֱלֹ־הֵיכֶם has a very precise connotation over and above — or, as we shall shortly see, probably as part of — its implication of kingship. For this we go to *Rashi* at *Exodus* 6:2. There God introduced himself to Moses with the words, אֲנִי ה'. *Rashi* remarks: I can be relied upon to reward those who serve me ... Now this is often the meaning of the phrase: אֲנִי ה': "I can be relied upon to punish" when the context requires this translation, or, "I can be relied upon to reward" when it is used in connection with the fulfillment of commandments ..."[3]

The coincidence of the idea of kingship and the dispensation of reward and punishment in the same phrase may be explained as follows.

Kingship as viewed by the Torah is that institution in which the administration of justice is rooted. Thus, for example, the elders of Israel when they came to to beg Samuel to proclaim a monarchy: *Grant us a king* so that he might judge us *so that we will be like all the nations*. And thus too the young Solomon's request at Giveon: *So grant Your servant a listening heart in order* to judge this people *to comprehend the difference between good and evil* (I Kings 3:9).

---

3. See *Maharal* in *Gur Aryeh* for three possible explanations of how the Sages read this idea into this phrase.

Justice posits accountability and accountability finds its most vivid and tangible expression in the rewards which await him who conscientiously performs his appointed tasks and in the punishments which are exacted for dereliction of duty and the perpetration of evil.

Accordingly we may say that the dispensation of reward and punishment which is implied in this phrase is a function of its broader meaning which proclaims God as king. אֲנִי ה׳ אֱל־הֵיכֶם describes God as a king who dispenses justice.

❁ ❁ ❁

Let us now move to a consideration of R' Yose ben Yehudah's contention that the juxtaposition of the phrase אֲנִי ה׳ אֱלֹהֵיכֶם to וְהָיוּ לָכֶם לְזִכָּרוֹן ... teaches that wherever *Zichronos* are mentioned they are to be accompanied by *Malchios*. How, in the light of what we have discussed, are we to understand this requirement?

In earlier essays we have noted that *Ramban* (*Drashah Le-Rosh Hashanah*) associates זָכְרוֹן with *judgment*. Accordingly wherever we encounter the concept of זִכָּרוֹן — be it during war [... וְנִזְכַּרְתֶּם לִפְנֵי ה׳ ... (*Numbers* 10:9)], be it as part of all our holy days [... וְהָיוּ לָכֶם לְזִכָּרוֹן (there, 10:10)] or on Rosh Hashanah [... זִכְרוֹן תְּרוּעָה (*Leviticus* 23:24)] we know that our fate is to hang in the balance.

Now the meting out of justice need not necessarily be associated with the concept of kingship. Judges, too, punish and occasionally reward. The word זָכְרוֹן by itself, even granting *Ramban's* assertion that it connotes justice, does not necessarily point to kingship.

Thus Rosh Hashanah might well have been a day of זִכְרוֹן תְּרוּעָה without in any way drawing upon the particular quality of God as King.

It is this misconception which R' Yose ben Yehudah's juxtaposition between זָכְרוֹן and מַלְכוּת seeks to expel. It teaches us that whenever God chooses to sit in judgment over us [זִכְרוֹנוֹת] we are to perceive that manifestation of His concern and interest as being anchored in the quality of kingship [מַלְכִיּוֹת] rather than in another relationship — such as that of judge — which might equally well have served.

We understand this requirement as follows:

The concept, judge, defines an activity not a relationship. The litigants or the accused who stand before a judge are passive. He is the repository and interpreter of the law, his decision binds and directs them, but it is not they whose obedience imbues him with the luster of his position, it is not his exercise of the judicial role which in any way gives body or meaning to their existence. A judge serves a system of justice.

Kingship is different. A king relates to the person. Kingship speaks of a symbiosis. אֵין מֶלֶךְ בְּלֹא עָם, *There can be no King without a people* (*Kad HaKemach, Rosh Hashanah*). King and people are defined, first and foremost, by an association rather than by specific roles. We cannot proclaim God as king, cannot relate to Him as king, without at the same time proclaiming ourselves as People. To experience God as King is to be transformed and inspired, to be imbued with a sense of infinite worth and with an awareness of a stern, demanding but withal, exhilarating, destiny.

I stand before a judge and feel powerless and worthless, pawn of a system which is blind to my individuality and interested only in its own perpetuation and validation. I stand before my King as Judge, and know that even if I will be found to have fallen short of my obligations He has cared for me, has sought my betterment, will punish my derelictions sternly and consistently — but will always have me, at the center of His concern.

It is this that R' Yose ben Yehudah has in mind when he teaches that *Zichronos* must always be accompanied by *Malchios*. God's judgment is to be savored as an event of personal significance of the highest order. It is to leave us — whatever the outcome — conscious of having been lifted, if only fleetingly, beyond the humdrum limitations of the finite. We have been summoned to render an accounting of our lives — and have touched eternity.

※ ※ ※

Earlier in this essay we noted that while *Zichronos* and *Shoforos* were rooted within the *parashah* of Rosh Hashanah, *Malchios* were not. They seemed, certainly according to R' Yose ben Yehudah, to be subsidiary to *Zichronos* rather than having a standing in their own right.

We have now learned otherwise. *Malchios* do not augment *Zichronos* but they define them. They lend *Zichronos* a specific nuance. They are an integral part of the day; more, they constitute its very essence. For the day is a day of זָכָרוֹן and *Malchios* speak of that relationship to God in which that זָכָרוֹן is to find ground and meaning. If the day is to be a day of זָכָרוֹן then it is — more basically and more fundamentally — to be a day of *Malchios*.

We began this essay by asking why the *kedushas hayom* blessing of Rosh Hashanah should speak of God's kingship. The answer has become clear. It is in that kingship in which the day's sanctity is rooted.

※ ※ ※

But why then are *Malchios* not mentioned in the *parashah* of Rosh Hashanah? Why, after all that we have learned, should the Torah not have included that too, directly in its description of the day?

Perhaps this is a part of the pattern of mystery which surrounds the Torah's treatment of Rosh Hashanah, of which we spoke above under *Today He Places All the Creatures of the World Before the Bar of Justice*.

We quote;

> Rosh Hashanah, from the very first moment that we meet up against it seems shrouded in mystery. *Now in*

the seventh month, on the first day of the month there shall occur for you a sacred convocation. It shall be for you a day of remembrance generated by a [shofar] blast. You shall perform no manner of work (Leviticus 23:23). We are given no hint at all to help us understand why this day among all others was chosen for singularity. What is to be *remembered*? Why by means of a [shofar] blast? And why, above all, on this particular day?

Rosh Hashanah is the only one of the *Yamim Tovim* which the Torah treats with such reticence. The time and content assigned to Pesach are self explanatory. Shavuos, while only its agricultural aspect is mentioned — never that at it's heart is the celebration of *Mattan Torah* — is tied to Pesach through the counting of the *Sefirah*, and thus a context is provided. There is no apparent logic mentioned in the Torah to the date assigned to Succos, but the idea of a *Yom Tov* devoted to the *contemplation* of our desert experiences is natural. The Torah identifies Yom Kippur as a day upon which God grants atonement for our sins and a simple computation using the dates given for God's appearance on Sinai and the giving of the *Luchos* provides an understanding for the special significance of the tenth of Tishrei.

But there is absolutely nothing in the Torah which would explain why any importance attaches to the *first day of the seventh month*, nor why or for what purpose the shofar is to be sounded on that day, nor, again, what *memory* is meant to be awakened.

The Oral Law, of course, fleshes out the written account. The date designated by the Torah is that of the Friday of creation, the day that man first appeared upon the earth. The [shofar] blast is to usher in the moment of God's awesome judgment — the accounting which he demands, upon this anniversary, of the use to which we have put this wonderful world which He so unstintingly gave us.

But of all this there is no hint at all in the written Torah.

It is as though the Torah as it is written [though, of course we know the reason from Torah Shebe'al Peh] wishes us to embark upon a journey of discovery, a searching for the essence and meaning of this day — and within that search, and as part of it, to burrow onwards and inwards into our own essence, until we have laid bare the meaning and implications of our own lives.

All this may also be true of the problem which we have now raised. By placing *Malchios* outside the *parashah* of *Rosh Hashanah* the Torah as it is written seems to be challenging us to discover the depths of the King/People relationship by our own initiative. We can leave Rosh Hashanah as simply a day of judgment and thereby deny ourselves the dimensions of the day which we have discovered in this essay. But — the way is open to explore further and deeper. We are free to turn the terror of retribution into a meeting with the Divine — and thereby unmask the *Yom Tov* potential which lies within this day of dread.

אַתָּה זוֹכֵר מַעֲשֵׂה עוֹלָם . . . ◆§
You Remember Actions Taken From the Beginning of Time

Language is our friend and our enemy. It frees us and it shackles us. It enables us to give body to our inchoate thoughts and feelings, but, because ultimately we cannot shake loose from its hold upon the concepts which it purports to describe, that body is often ill-formed or misformed, projecting an image which falls woefully short of an accurate depiction of reality.

We know, or think we know, what we mean when we talk about remembering. We remember people who have crossed our paths, events which have long since passed into history. Our mind's eye sees them through the haze generated by millions of unrelated experiences, filters them through the accepting and rejecting mechanisms of our minds. They are murky images subjectively remembered — and subjectively distorted.

And so, because we are in thrall to our language, we tend to think of God's remembering in similar terms. We — so we would like to think — are at the sharply focused center of His awareness. The actions taken from the beginning of time form an unobtrusive background which, in the final analysis matters very little. They are, after all, only dim — memories.

This is what we would tend to think. The truth, of course, is very different — and its implications must rattle and shake us out of our equanimity. God's memory is not a *memory* at all. There is no past, there is no present, there is no future. There is only a sharp relentless looking which illuminates the totality of existence with the dreadful clarity of immediacy, and comprehends the billions who live and who have lived, in one penetrating gaze, which inhibits their individuality not at all. There are no shadows to offer even the illusion of anonymity, no crowds into which to blend. We, in our ridiculous and shameful puniness must, as it were, rub shoulders with — and must stand comparison to — the Chafetz Chaim, Rabbi Akiva and indeed the *Avos*.

Memory — God's memory — is a frightening thing indeed.

❅ ❅ ❅

What precisely does God remember?

The wording of the *Zichronos* blessing leaves us with a difficulty which we do not encounter in the case of *Malchios* or *Shoforos*.

Let us digress for a moment and discuss the nature and structure of the *berachos*, the blessings, which are the building blocks of our prayers. Naturally we expect their structure to be determined by an inner logic which produces a cohesive whole. We expect it to progress naturally from an introduction [פְּתִיחָה, *pesichah*], to a climax [חֲתִימָה, *chasimah*] — and that it all be of one piece, concerned with one unified topic.

Malchios and *Shoforos* are constructed in precisely this way. Each has an opening passage which elaborates upon the theme which informs the entire blessing and which is expressed in its *chasimah*. In the case of *Malchios* the theme is God's kingship and the ending reads, ... *King of the whole universe* .... In the case of *Shoforos* it is the central role which the shofar has played at various watershed events in Jewish history, and this leads to the *chasimah*: *Who hears the teruah sounds of His people, Israel, with mercy.*

Zichronos — unexpectedly — is different. There is, indeed, a long introductory passage which describes in lavish detail how God, as He sits in judgment over us, is aware of — "remembers" — every last detail of all that we have done. How He knows our thoughts and our dreams, our ambitions and our plottings, how

He charts in exquisite and terrifying detail the conscious and unconscious drives which precipitated our decisions, the intended and unintended repercussions of all that we accomplished and perpetrated. It speaks of the fates of individuals and entire peoples hanging in the balance, evokes the terror of a confrontation with oneself and with one's God — one which cannot be escaped.

But is all this really what is meant when the Sages bid us to say *Zichronos* on Rosh Hashanah, ... *so that your memory might come before Me for your advantage (Rosh Hashanah 16a)*?

Not if we take the *chasimah* of *Zichronos* as our guide. This final blessing speaks only of God remembering the covenant which He concluded with us [זוֹכֵר הַבְּרִית] and not at all of Him as a judge, remembering our deeds and misdeeds. Indeed none of the ten verses which form the bulk of the *Zichronos* blessing seem to echo the theme of the introductory passage. So too, the concluding section which leads up to the *chasimah* focuses solely upon the fulfillment of our historic and messianic destiny and, within that context, asks that God *remember* the *Akeidah*, the binding of our father Isaac, which is the bedrock upon which the foundation of the uniqueness of our national relationship with God is grounded. Nothing at all is said about Rosh Hashanah as a day of judgment, nothing about the awesome detail in which our innermost lives lie bare before God's all-seeing eye.

We look in our *machzor* and are confused. We do not see what precisely it is that we would have God remember. Where, having declared God as King through the recitation of *Malchios* are we to head? Are we to tremble before God as Judge or to exult before God as the caring loving Mover of history Who will — we know it absolutely — guide our march through history towards the fulfillment of our destiny?

❈ ❈ ❈

Let us examine the Mishnah in *Rosh Hashanah* 16a — which draws our attention to Rosh Hashanah as a day of judgment — in the light of what the Gemara has to say about it.

The Mishnah reads as follows:

> At four junctures [of the year] the world is judged:... On Rosh Hashanah all who walk the earth pass before Him like young sheep, as it said (*Psalms* 33:15) *Who fashions all their hearts together, Who understands all their deeds*...

Now it is clear that when the Mishnah uses the metaphor of the *young sheep*, the intent is to illustrate that each of us must face the judgment of Rosh Hashanah as individuals. Just as *young sheep* are counted singly as they pass through the gate of the coral, so too is each person judged alone and not as an anonymous cipher within a crowd. In fact, the Gemara offers two more explanations for the term, בְּנֵי מָרוֹן which we translated as *young sheep*. One is, *like soldiers who pass in file before the king*, another, *like climbers of a particularly steep mountain pass who must make their progress in single file*.

Even without discussing how each of these metaphors differs in its message from the others, we can appreciate the underlying principle which is common to all of them: We are to bear responsibility for our actions as individuals. Each of us, as a discrete personality, is the object of God's scrutiny.

All the stranger, then, to learn at *Rosh Hashanah* 18a that R' Yochanan taught that, while, as our Mishnah has taught, each person must pass singly before God, still, כּוּלָן נִסְקָרִים בִּסְקִירָה אַחַת, *They are all apprehended [by God] in one comprehensive vision*.

What is being said here? Why make the point that God sees the entire world in one all-comprehending glance when the Mishnah so clearly wishes to stress the opposite idea — namely that each of us must face judgment as an individual?

We suspect that the correct understanding of R' Yochanan's statement may be the key to solving the problem which we had with the wording of the *Zichronos* blessing.

The reading of the *chasimah* of *Zichronos* makes it clear that the object of God's זִכָּרוֹן [read, *judgment* according to *Ramban* whom we have quoted on a number of occasions] on Rosh Hashanah is the community rather than the individual. God *remembers* His בְּרִית, His *covenant* — and that covenant was concluded with the nation, not with the individual.

We can understand this well when we consider the midrashic teaching that the judgment of Rosh Hashanah is grounded in the first judgment which occurred on that day — that which determined the fate of the very first man: God said to Adam, "Adam, you are to serve as a paradigm for your children. Just as you stood before me accused on this day and were treated with mercy. So too will your children stand accused before Me on this day, and they too will be treated with mercy." (*Yalkut Shimoni Pinchas* 381).

It is כְּלַל יִשְׂרָאֵל, the nation of Israel, which became the later-day "Adam" of mankind [אַתֶּם קְרוּיִין אָדָם וְאֵין עכּוּם קְרוּיִין אָדָם) (*Yevamos* 61a)]. Adam was paradigm for "Adam". It is to the People of Israel, partners in God's covenant, that the זִכָּרוֹן of Rosh Hashanah is directed.

Jewish essence [חֵלֶק לְעוֹלָם הַבָּא, the right to expect a *portion in Olam Haba, the World-to-Come*] is predicated upon the sharing in the joys and pains of Jewish peoplehood. We quote *Rambam, Hilchos Teshuvah* 3:10:

> He who sets himself apart from communal involvement [דַּרְכֵי הַצִּבּוּר] even if he committed no sins at all; only that he is separate from the community of Israel, does not fulfill *mitzvos* as a part of them, does not get involved in their sorrows nor fast on their fast-days; but goes in his own way as would one of the gentiles, as though he were no part of them. He has no portion in the World-to-Come.

Accordingly we may assume that the judgment to which the individual is exposed on Rosh Hashanah at least as far as the Jewish people, bearers of the *covenant* is concerned, seeks to probe the extent to which his acts of omission and commission mark him as a loyal son of his people or as a renegade who has forfeited his right to be counted among them. It is perhaps this which R' Yochanan had in mind when he taught that although we must face judgment as individuals we are all comprehended in one glance. The background against which the judgment of Rosh Hashanah takes place is the peoplehood of Israel, that entity with which God forged His covenant. All of us, we who are currently the bearers of Jewish destiny together with generations yet unborn and with those who have long since passed into history, are comprehended in God's all-seeing and all-knowing glance. On the day of Adam's creation it is to that "Adam" that God's attention is turned. And each of us — singly, unhelped and unprotected by the anonymity of the crowds must give an accounting of his deeds so that he might claim to be part of that entity.

The wording of the *Zichronos* blessing which perturbed us before is really no more than a reflection of the Mishnah and the Gemara which we have now discussed. The introduction pictures in graphic and frightening detail the dread of a judgment which must be faced — alone. The section which leads up to the *chasimah* together with the זוֹכֵר הַבְּרִית ending, reflects R' Yochanan's teaching and takes us, as it were, beneath the surface of what is happening. In the final analysis it is God's determination to breath life into His covenant with Israel which gives Rosh Hashanah its character as a יוֹם הַזִּכָּרוֹן.

... וּבְקוֹל שֹׁפָר עֲלֵיהֶם הוֹפָעְתָּ ... ~§
... And Accompanied By a Shofar Blast Did You Appear to Them ...

The מִצְוַת הַיּוֹם of Rosh Hashanah, that which defines the day and lends it focus, is the blowing of the shofar. We could say that the shofar is to Rosh Hashanah what *matzah* is to Pesach, the *lulav* and *esrog* is to Succos and fasting is to Yom Kippur.

But, there is a difference. The three examples which we adduced are all appropriate to the times with which they are associated. *Matzah*, the *bread of affliction* reminds us of the slavery in Egypt, the *lulav* and *esrog* are chosen by the Torah as agricultural produce with which to *rejoice before God* on a harvest festival (*Leviticus* 23:39-40), and fasting is natural to a day of *atonement*.

But what is the function of the shofar? And why is that function appropriate to Rosh Hashanah?

We quote *Rambam*, *Hilchos Teshuvah* 3:4.

> Although the obligation to blow the shofar on Rosh Hashanah is mandated by the Torah [גְּזֵרַת הַכָּתוּב and we are therefore not called upon to find a reason for it], still it hints [at a message.]
>
> It is as though the shofar calls out to us, "Wake up you sleepers from your sleep, and those who slumber be aroused from your stupor. Examine your deeds, do *teshuvah* and remember your Creator.
>
> This is addressed to those who allow fripperies of passing fashion to cause them to forget the truth and who foolishly spend their time on vanities and emptiness which have no use at all.
>
> [It calls to them] 'Take heed of your own souls, make sure that what you do and what you plan be positive. Stop walking the paths of evil ...'

מלכיות, זכרונות, שופרות — *Herald of Royalty*

What is the relationship between the mandated *mitzvah* for which we cannot expect to know a reason, and the message at which it hints? Is a hint meaningful if, for all we know, it has absolutely no connection with the essential nature of what we are doing?

It seems much more likely that the message at which the shofar hints is a natural outgrowth of its essential nature.

Let us then try to analyze what precisely a shofar is meant to do.

As a point of departure we can go to *Rosh Hashanah* 26a. There the Gemara defines the function of *shofar* as זִכָּרוֹן, a means of stimulating *memory* or *awareness*.

The Gemara offers this definition in the context of a discussion concerning the disqualification of a shofar made of the horns of a cow. The Gemara had suggested that such a shofar cannot be used because of the principle that אֵין קָטֵגוֹר נַעֲשֶׂה סָנֵיגוֹר, *a prosecutor cannot speak for the defense*. Anything that is closely associated with our shortcomings [and thus a "prosecutor'] must, where the need is to bring our merits to the fore [speaking for the defense], be disqualified. The cow's horn would recall the terrible sin of the *golden calf*.

The Gemara had found this principle invoked to explain why the *Kohen Gadol* had to change into *white vestments* [בִּגְדֵי לָבָן] before entering the Holy of Holies as part of the Yom Kippur service. His normal vestments contained gold, and gold invites reference to the *golden* calf. It has the character of *prosecutor*.

Now, since for all the portions of the service which were performed outside the Holy of Holies the *Kohen Gadol* wore his golden vestments, and since, moreover. the ark in which the stone tablets reposed was made of gold even though it was placed within the Holy of Holies, it is clear that for the principle of אֵין קָטֵגוֹר נַעֲשֶׂה סָנֵיגוֹר to apply, two conditions must be fulfilled: The unit concerned must be involved actively in an act of service [the clothes worn by the *Kohen* who *does* the service, and not the passive ark] and the service must take place in the Holy of Holies.

Given this second limitation, the Gemara is puzzled. Why should a cow's horn be disqualified for the shofar of Rosh Hashanah? Manifestly the shofar is not blown in the Holy of Holies?

To this the Gemara answers: כֵּיוָן דְלְזִכָּרוֹן הוּא כְּבִפְנִים דָּמִי, *Because the shofar's function is to generate* זִכָּרוֹן, *it has the character of taking place within [the Holy of Holies].*

We may, for the moment, leave aside the question of why the concept of זִכָּרוֹן should be associated with the Holy of Holies. For our purpose it is sufficient to have recognized that the function which the Gemara assigns to the shofar is one of generating זִכָּרוֹן.

Now the Gemara would seem to have two possible sources for its assertion. There is, of course, the expression, זִכְרוֹן תְּרוּעָה which the Torah uses when it speaks of Rosh Hashanah at *Leviticus* 23:24. But that phrase does not tell us why there is such a connection. For that we must go to the silver trumpets [חֲצוֹצְרֹת] which Moses was commanded to make at *Numbers* 10:1-10.

Accordingly we will now move to a consideration of that *parashah*.[1]

---

1. The legitimacy of comparing the function of the shofar to that of the *chatzotzros* is based upon the Mishnah in *Rosh Hashanah* 26b.

> Two *chatzotzros* were positioned on the sides [of the shofar]. The shofar blast was drawn out longer while that of the *chatzotzros* was shorter, because the actual *mitzvah* of the day [of Rosh Hashanah] is performed with the shofar.
>
> On fast-days two *chatzotzros* were positioned in the middle. The shofar blast was shorter and that of the *chatzotzros* was longer because the actual *mitzvah* of the day [of fasting] is performed with the *chatzotzros*.

The Gemara (27a) explains that the usage of having the shofar surrounded by, and sounded together with, *chatzotzros*, was limited to the Temple. The requirement that both instruments be employed together is based on *Psalms* 98:6: *With chatzotzros and shofar sound, call out before the King,* HASHEM. Only *before the King,* HASHEM, that is, as part of the Temple service, are both to be used. But, be that as it may, and however circumscribed the application of the requirement that the two instruments be played together may be, we do see that shofar and *chatzotzros* belong within the same category.

> ... Make for yourself two *chatzotzros* of silver — you shall beat them out — and they shall serve you as a means of summoning the people and to start the camps upon their journeys.
>
> They shall blow a *tekiah* upon them, and the entire congregation shall meet with you at the entrance of the Tent of Meeting.
>
> If only one is blown then the princes, leaders of Israel's thousands, shall meet with you.
>
> Now when you blow a *teruah* then the encampments which dwell to the east shall begin to travel.
>
> Then you shall blow a second *teruah* ... a *teruah* shall be sounded so that they begin to travel.
>
> But when the congregation is to gather, a *tekiah* shall be sounded but not a *teruah*.
>
> ... Now when you go to war in your land against an enemy who oppresses you, then you shall blow a *teruah* on the *chatzotzros*, and thus you will be remembered before HASHEM your God and be saved from your enemies.
>
> And on the days of your rejoicing and upon your appointed times and on *Rosh Chodesh*, then you shall blow a *tekiah* on the *chatzotzros* as you bring your burnt offerings ...and they shall serve as a remembrance before your God. I am HASHEM your God.

A careful reading of the passage yields the following: The *chatzotzros* were manufactured *as a means of summoning the people and to start the camps upon their journeys*. They were also to be used during battle and on the Holy days. But this use is not presented as the reason for which they were made. They were *made* to summon the people as needed and to send them upon their travels, they were also *used* to elicit זָכָרוֹן in times of need and joy.

We could formulate this insight as follows: God's זָכָרוֹן is, so to speak, aroused when those *chatzotzros*, the purpose of which it is to summon the people and to set them upon their journeys, are sounded. זִכָּרוֹן, then, would be the awareness of Israel's readiness to answer the call, their willingness to shoulder responsibility, their eagerness to embark upon the perils of the unknown — because it is their God Who has called them to the fulfillment of their destiny.

Let us see how this works in practice.

An enemy comes to oppress us in our land. Our armies mass to defend us from the oppressor. What are the thoughts which should animate the Jewish soldier preparing himself for battle? Let us listen to *Rambam* (*Melachim* 7:15).

> ... Once he enters the thick of the battle let him put his trust in Him Who is Israel's hope and the One Who saves them in times of trouble. Let him realize that he is waging war to assert the Oneness of God and let him therefore be willing to lay down his life without fear or terror. Let him think neither of his wife nor of his children ... but let his mind be focused upon the sanctification of God's Name ...

Well and good. But easier in theory than in practice. Fear's icy tentacles clutch at the soldier's heart. Terror smothers him in its deadly embrace, seeps into every pore, paralyzes and stultifies.

What is he to do?

What makes us afraid in the face of danger?

> A student was following R' Yishmael ben R' Yose in the streets of Zion. [R' Yishmael] noticed that [the student] was afraid. He said to him, "You are a sinner!" For it is written: *Sinners in Zion are frightened* (Isaiah 33:14) (*Berachos* 60a).

It is sin which makes us cowards. Sin, which robs us of our self-esteem, drains us of our courage.

מלכיות, זכרונות, שופרות — *Herald of Royalty*

Let us once more turn to *Rambam*, this time in *Taanis* 1:1 where he explains, based upon our passage in *Numbers*, why the *chatzotzros* were to be blown in times of national disaster.

> The Torah obliges us to call out and to blow the *teruah* on *chatzotzros* whenever tragedy strikes our people. This, as it is written, ... *against the enemy who comes to oppress you, you shall blow a teruah upon the chatzotzros*. This teaches that any disaster which threatens us, such as famine, plague, locusts and the like, we are to call out and to blow a *teruah*.
>
> This, as part of the process of *teshuvah*. For, when trouble comes and people call out and blow the *teruah*, everyone will realize that it was brought on by their evil deeds ... and this realization will bring relief.
>
> But, if they do not call out and do not blow the *teruah*, but insist that what occurred came about through natural causes, ... this will result in their clinging to their evil ways ...

The sequence is clear. The *chatzotzros* are blown, calling to introspection and the need to distance oneself from all that is base and unholy, to goad us into reaching for that purity of heart and spirit which alone can drive away the cloying shackles of fear. That done, the way is open to an appreciation of our exalted destiny, the awareness that our wars are God's wars, our victories a proclamation of קִדּוּשׁ הַשֵּׁם, *the sanctification of God's Name*. Soldiers marching into battle secure in this knowledge can be sure that they will be *remembered* by God [... וְנִזְכַּרְתֶּם] Who will save them from their enemies.

A similar function can readily be assigned to the *chatzotzros* which are to accompany the offering of the sacrifices on, ... *the days of your rejoicing and upon your appointed times and on Rosh Chodesh*. Our Holy Days [with the exception of *Rosh Chodesh*] are called, מוֹעֵד [from וַעַד, *to meet*], an opportunity to *meet* with God, to renew that relationship of love and caring which animated those periods in history which they recall. They are מִקְרָא קֹדֶשׁ, a *calling to sanctity*, moments of intense religious experience. They seek to generate an intimacy born of joy, to celebrate the unison between Israel and its God which grows from a congruence of aspirations and goals. These are days like no other; they insist that we approach them with a full and realized awareness of who and what we are. To paraphrase Hillel: If *we* are here, if our sense of history and destiny is alive and pulsating, then everything is here. Absent that *we* — there is nothing here at all.

And so — the shofar call must summon us and set us upon our path. As we bring our historical sensitivity, *ourselves*, to the celebration, our זִכָּרוֹן rises up before our God. As we have remembered so does He, so to speak, remember, and the מוֹעֵד, the *meeting*, aspect of the *Yom Tov* is consummated.

We are now ready to return to *Rambam's* discussion of the function which the shofar is to play on Rosh Hashanah. Certainly the obligation to sound the shofar on the *first day of the seventh month* is a גְּזֵרַת הַכָּתוּב, a *mitzvah* mandated by the Torah for which we *know* no reason. As we have pointed out so many times before, the Torah's presentation of this day is shrouded in mystery. We are told nothing at all about its significance, nor why it should be a day of זִכְרוֹן תְּרוּעָה. In this sense it is a גְּזֵרַת הַכָּתוּב. But the message to which it *hints* is of a piece with the general function of the shofar. It is there to call us to our posts. In this case it is meant to jolt the sleepers and the slumberers from their equanimity, to force them to focus upon opportunities forever lost, upon moments of potential which can never be recovered.

Once more, the shofar summons us and sets us upon our path. There is a past which must, to the extent possible, be recovered, a future which may yet be our's if we but listen to its call.

מלכיות, זכרונות, שופרות — *Herald of Royalty*

❅ ❅ ❅

At the beginning of this essay we discussed *Rosh Hashanah* 26a where the Gemara maintains that the shofar, כֵּיוָן דְּלְזִכָּרוֹן הוּא כִּבְפָנִים דָּמִי, *because its function is to generate* זִכָּרוֹן, *has the character of taking place within [the Holy of Holies].*

Let us try to understand why this should be so.

What, precisely, are the salient features of the Holy of Holies?

The Holy of Holies is located in our world but is not of a piece with it. *Bava Basra* 99a teaches that, מְקוֹם אָרוֹן וּכְרוּבִים אֵינוֹ מִן הַמִּדָּה, neither the ark nor the angelic figures which Solomon erected within the Holy of Holies, took up any space. That is, there remained as much empty room as there would have been had the ark and the *Keruvim* not existed. Whatever else is implied this certainly means that the Holy of Holies was not subject to the spatial constraints of an ordinary, physical area.

More.

The Sages taught that each of the vestments worn by the *Kohen Gadol* had the power to atone for certain of Israel's sins. The מְעִיל, the *cloak* which he wore while performing the Divine service throughout the year, had the function of eliciting forgiveness for the sin of לָשׁוֹן הָרַע, the evil gossip to which we are all so prone. But, it could only atone for this sin in its crassest, most blatant form. אֲבַק לָשׁוֹן הָרַע, literally, *the dust of evil gossip*, that is the kind of gossip which is not expressly evil but nevertheless by nuance conveys something negative about our fellow man, can find no atonement — until the *Kohen Gadol* enters the Holy of Holies on Yom Kippur.

Why?

Maharal explains. *Bava Basra* 165a quotes a shocking statement in the name of Rav: הַכֹּל בְּלָשׁוֹן הָרַע, *every single person*, without exception occasionally indulges in evil gossip. The Gemara cannot accept this. Is it possible, the Gemara asks, that no one can avoid this terrible sin? In response, the Gemara modifies the original statement. Rav had not said, בְּלָשׁוֹן הָרַע, but,

בְּאַבַק לָשׁוֹן הָרַע. Certainly, people who live responsibly can make the effort to avoid real לָשׁוֹן הָרַע. But, אֲבַק לָשׁוֹן הָרַע is something else. It is simply part of the human condition — and this with no exceptions at all — to, occasionally, say something which, at least, hints at the disparagement of another.

If so, *Maharal* argues, then *for human beings* there can be no atonement for this sin. If indeed it is endemic to the human condition, how, as long as we remain human, can it possibly be eradicated?

It is for this reason that atonement must wait until the *Kohen Gadol* enters the Holy of Holies on Yom Kippur. At that moment he, as it were, sheds his human limitations, becomes more angel than man. It is, in a real sense, a moment of truth — the truth of Jewish goodness, the truth which maintains that our limitations and insignificancies are coincidental to the surface of life. That, at its essential level we can be, indeed are, free of even that pettiness from which the propensity for אֲבַק לָשׁוֹן הָרַע grows.

The Holy of Holies, then, is the place in which, if only fleetingly, our true selves, untainted by the dross of every-day living, are revealed.

The shofar blast on Rosh Hashanah achieves a similar result. As we saw above, it calls us to once more discover our essential nature, to bring all that we ever were, all that we are capable of being, all that dreams and unflagging energy can make of ourselves to come before our God. It dares us to undertake the daunting trek into the unknown and unknowable future. It challenges us to follow our destiny, wherever it might lead. It demands that we break with the known and the comfortable as we once broke camp in the wilderness; that we discover God's will for our future and that therein — we discover ourselves.

At its insistent and portentous summons, smallness must peel away and our essence, forged through the dreadful fires of our history, comes to the fore. We are to discover that we are not, or need not be, of this world; that the filth which encrusts us is only surface deep and that though we might appear discolored like the *tents of Kedar* we need only submit to a thorough cleansing to once more glisten white like the *curtains of Solomon* (*Shir HaShirim* 1:5).

A shofar made from a cow's horn, recalling as it does the dreadful sin of the Golden Calf, is simply inappropriate in such a setting. That blotch upon our history was an aberration which never expressed our true selves. To invoke its memory would indeed serve as a fearsome accusation, but — it would be hurled at the wrong party. The true *we* was not involved. The shofar blast, if only for a moment, reveals us as we really are. We are our own best סָנֵיגוֹר.

❈ ❈ ❈

We headed this essay with a quote from the *Shofros* blessing which begins by recalling the Sinaitic experience. From there, by way of the ten mandatory verses, it moves on and reaches its climax in a longing glance towards the future: *Our God and the God of our fathers, O sound the Great Shofar for our freedom....*

The shofar of Sinai and the shofar of the Messiah. These appear to be the stuff out of which the *Shofros* blessing of Rosh Hashanah is made.

But why? What possible bearing do these mighty — and supernatural — blasts have upon our much more modest efforts on Rosh Hashanah?

The answer is both shockingly simple — and overwhelming in its implications.

The shofar of Rosh Hashanah is an echo of the shofar-blast of Sinai, it anticipates the *Great Shofar* of the Messiah.

All these blasts are essentially the same. All beg us to gather to their call. All, having successfully summoned us, send us triumphantly upon the path which God has chosen for us.

God at Sinai would not have trusted us with His Torah had the dread call of the shofar not first shaken us out of our ordinariness, had it not forced us to find — and glory in — our essence, had it not hinted at the cataclysmic trek through history, which, as carriers of God's truth we would be forced to undertake — and had we not responded to its call with the quiet heroism of our נַעֲשֶׂה וְנִשְׁמַע.

Mashiach will not come to take us home in order that we should bring with us the grotesque malformations of character and value-systems with which our exile has turned us into caricatures of what we really are. The Great Shofar which will herald his coming will be the greatest summoning of all. Its shattering sound will crash through the terrible layers of inauthenticity with which our essential life-force has been distorted. It will, by the time it reaches our hearts, have become a sweet caress of comfort, a loving assurance that, after all, we have survived, that we matter, that we have a future, that, above all, we are good. It, too, will set us upon a path. Where it will lead we cannot now know, what it will demand we can only guess. But it will lead upward and onward into God's embrace.

All this, and more, lies hidden in the shofar of Rosh Hashanah. Upon its sound we are wafted into the Holy of Holies, stripped of physical constraints of time and place. Past and future fuse into the inexpressible reality of the moment. Silent and submissive we offer our poor lives for inspection. The picture may not be pleasant. There may be much that is ugly, much that is stunted. But it is all that we have to offer to God. We give it freely. And as we give it we make a whispered promise to improve. We ourselves may hear this promise and mean it only imperfectly. But, upon the shofar-blast, it rises up to God — and finds Him upon the Throne of Mercy.

Yom HaKippurim
יום הכיפורים

וְנִסְלַח לְכָל עֲדַת בְּנֵי יִשְׂרָאֵל...
The Entire Family of Israel Shall Be Forgiven...

The recitation of this verse as part of the *Kol Nidrei* service, is something of a mystery. It is a quote from *Numbers* 15:26 where it promises atonement in the event that an entire community inadvertently committed idol-worship. Certain sacrifices are to be brought, and when that has been done, the people are forgiven.

Clearly that is not what we have in mind on *Kol Nidrei* night, and we must assume that the verse was borrowed from its original setting because the wording was deemed appropriate for the context in which it appears here [1]

Why then do we recite this verse?

The answer to this question, depends directly upon the wording of the *Kol Nidrei* passage. There is a disagreement among the commentators whether it is meant to annul any vows which had been made during the previous year retroactively, or whether it is a declaration of intent that any future vows should not be valid.

According to the first view it is simple to understand the purpose of the, וְנִסְלַח... verse. It affirms that, now that the

---

1. Liturgical needs which invest verses with meanings different from those which they carried in their original, Biblical, context, are not uncommon.

For example, בָּרוּךְ כְּבוֹד ה׳ מִמְּקוֹמוֹ in the *Kedushah* has a different meaning than it carried in the original *Ezekiel* passage. So too, וְזֹאת הַתּוֹרָה .... in the original *Va'eschanan* verse, does not connote the Sefer Torah which we have in mind during *hagbahah*.

Indeed, even the קַבָּלַת עוֹל מַלְכוּת שָׁמַיִם which we read into our twice daily recitation of ... שְׁמַע יִשְׂרָאֵל, does not inhere in the words as they were originally said by Moses — see *Rashi*, there.

Kol Nidrei — כל נדרי

previous year's vows have been annulled, forgiveness may be expected if, by chance, they were transgressed.

But — what forgiveness is required if we are simply making a pronouncement concerning future vows?

Rosh recognizes the difficulty and thinks that, with the וְנִסְלַח... verse we might be asking for forgiveness in anticipation of future infringements. But *Gra* is uncomfortable with this solution. It hardly appears logical to beg indulgence for sins as yet uncommitted [קָשֶׁה לְהוֹלְמוֹ שֶׁיְבַקֵּשׁ סְלִיחָה עַל עֲוֹנוֹת שֶׁיַּעֲשֶׂה לְהַבָּא].

For us the problem is acute. Our version of *Kol Nidrei* — ... *from this Yom Kippur until the next Yom Kippur* ... — clearly accords with the second opinion. Given this, and accepting *Gra's* hesitation concerning *Rosh's* solution, what is our understanding of the ...וְנִסְלַח passage?

When we consider that the ...וְנִסְלַח verse is followed directly by, ...סְלַח נָא which culminates in God's promise: סָלַחְתִּי כִּדְבָרֶיךָ, and that this passage seems to be quite independent of the *Kol Nidrei* proclamation, we may suggest that וְנִסְלַח, too, is separate from *Kol Nidrei* and should be read together with סְלַח נָא...

If our thesis is correct we are faced with two tasks. First, we will have to analyze the thought which runs through this, now expanded, passage as a discrete unit. Then we will need to locate it logically within the context in which it occurs. We are certainly justified in assuming that the sequence: כָּל נִדְרֵי ...„ עַל דַּעַת הַמָּקוֹם ...וְנִסְלַח has some unifying theme which makes it an appropriate introduction to the *maariv* of Yom Kippur.

❦ ❦ ❦

First, then, the ...וְנִסְלַח section.

The passage, as we have understood it, begins with ...וְנִסְלַח, — a statement that the Congregation of Israel had won forgiveness because,... *all the people had acted inadvertently* [כִּי לְכָל הָעָם בִּשְׁגָגָה]; it continues with Moses' request [after the debacle of the spies] that God, *forgive the sins of His people as He had borne their importunings from the moment that they had left Egypt up to the present time*; and culminates with God's assurance that He had forgiven them, *in accordance with the argument which Moses had made* [סָלַחְתִּי כִּדְבָרֶיךָ]. See *Rashi* there — ... בִּשְׁבִיל מַה שֶׁאָמַרְתָּ מִבִּלְתִּי יְכוֹלֶת.

How are we to understand these three components as they interact with one another in the context of this introductory segment to the *maariv* of Yom Kippur?

First, the statement that Israel *has* been forgiven because it has acted inadvertently. In its original context this verse makes perfect sense. It is borrowed from a section which describes a case in which the entire people had been inveigled into an act of idol-worship by a mistaken ruling of the *Sanhedrin*. The people followed the ruling, unaware that it had been made in error. The Torah provides for atonement for this *inadvertent* transgression through certain communal sacrifices. All is simple and entirely logical. But, how can this verse, which expressly ties the atonement to the fact that the transgressions had been *inadvertent* be used to typify the atonement of Yom Kippur, which, the requisite *teshuvah* having been undertaken, certainly atones even for such sins as were committed intentionally?[2]

We might eliminate this difficulty by referring to *Yoma* 86b where Reish Lakish teaches that any *teshuvah*, even one which was not undertaken altruistically out of love for God, but simply out of fear of the terrible consequences of sin, will turn זְדוֹנוֹת, *sins*

---

2. We have stated, ... upon the requisite *teshuvah*, because, since the destruction of the Temple and the consequent elimination of the sacrificial service, *teshuvah* is indeed required if Yom Kippur is to atone — see *Rambam Hilchos Teshuvah* 1:3. However, in earlier times, when the *Sa'ir HaMishtale'ach* was still brought, it atoned for certain classes of transgressions even without *teshuvah*. For details, see *Rambam, Hilchos Teshuvah* 1:2.

The first explanation of the appropriateness of the ... וְנִסְלַח verse which we offer within, would not be correct in a situation in which no *teshuvah* would be required. But, needless to say, there is no indication that this verse was used at the time when the Temple was still standing.

committed purposefully, into שְׁגָגוֹת, sins committed without intention.

Thus, since as we noted above, Yom Kippur — bereft of the Temple service — atones only when accompanied by *teshuvah*, the sins of which we are cleansed are indeed ones which have the character of having been committed inadvertently. For, even if at the time, the action was fully intended, the *teshuvah* has the mitigating ability to turn it into *shogeg*.

But — we need to pursue this idea a little further. The answer appears a little too pat. By what legerdemain are purposeful transgressions transformed into unintended ones? And, if they are, why is this concept so central to the idea of Yom Kippur that we should give it pride of place at the start of Yom Kippur, before we have even begun the formal *maariv*?

There are two passages in the Gemara which can help throw light upon our problems. The first which we will consider is in *Shabbos* 89b.

> ... The time will come when God will say to Abraham, "Your children have sinned!" He will answer, "O Master of the World, let them be destroyed for the greater sanctification of Your name."
>
> God will say to Himself, "Let Me tell this to Jacob who had to suffer through the raising of his children. Perhaps he will ask mercy for them."
>
> He said to him, "Your children have sinned!" He answered, "O Master of the World, let them be destroyed for the greater sanctification of Your name."
>
> God will say, "The older one [Abraham] has no feeling, the younger one [Jacob] can proffer no advice.
>
> He said to Isaac, "Your children have sinned!"
>
> He answered, "Are they my children and not Yours? ... And furthermore, how long does man live? Seventy years. Take off twenty-five of those seventy for the nights [when people are asleep and not

sinning.] Only twenty-five are left. Take off twelve-and-a-half spent in prayer, eating and eliminating so that only twelve-and-a-half are left. If you are willing to bear [the sins committed during] all of this time, well and good. If not, I will bear half, and do You bear the other half. And even if You will insist that I bear them all, I did, after all, sacrifice myself before You . . .

Clearly, there is much in this *aggadah* which needs explaining. A detailed analysis is not appropriate to this context. But Isaac's offer to go, as it were, half and half with God is vastly germane to our agenda. What precisely did Isaac mean by this astounding offer?

Commentators explain as follows: Both God and Isaac must, as it were, bear responsibility for Israel's sins. It is God Who imbued us with the *Yetzer HaRa*, the evil inclination which makes it so difficult for us to maintain our virtue. It is Isaac, who, by blessing Esau, condemned us to the bitter years of exile which have done so much to erode our sanctity and to make us prone to sin. It is only fair that, between them, they carry the burden of our wrongdoing.

Again there is much here which we could profitably examine. But, within the confines of our current field of interest, we limit ourselves to the truly shocking assumption that God Himself is somehow to blame for our sins because He gave us our *Yetzer HaRa*. What does this mean? Surely we are expected to control ourselves. How can we possibly blame God for our weakness.

There is another Gemara which is germane to our discussion and we cite it herewith. It comes from *Yoma* 19b where Abba Shaul relates that it was the custom throughout *Eretz Yisrael* to stay awake on the night of Yom Kippur. The *Kohen Gadol* was forbidden to sleep on this night and people wanted to be associated with his vigil. However, many people were unable to use this additional time constructively and ended up sinning. The Gemara tells that Eliyahu HaNavi said to R' Yehudah:

You ask why *Mashiach* does not come. [I will tell you.] Tonight is Yom Kippur and a number of young women have been violated in Nehardai.

[R' Yehudah] asked him, "What does God say to this?"

He answered, *"Sin crouches at the door"* [The *Yetzer HaRa* forces people into transgression (they are not to blame) *Rashi*].

"And how does the Satan respond to this?"

He answered, "On Yom Kippur the Satan is not permitted to accuse.'

Whatever else this cryptic story is meant to convey, it most certainly makes the point that sin is foreign to us. Were it not for the accusatory function of the Satan, then God, left, as it were, to Himself, would never blame us for our sins. He would always excuse us by maintaining that we were coerced by our *Yetzer Hara*. It is the Satan who, during the rest of the year, insists that we are not to get off so easily. But — and here, for us, is the significant point — on Yom Kippur, the Satan must be silent.

The relevance of this Gemara to the one we cited above is clear. Both maintain that Jewish sin is somehow an aberration. The *Yetzer Hara*, not we, is somehow the culprit. Rather than being identified with our baser instincts, he is an antagonist from without, against whose blandishments we are considered, at least on Yom Kippur when the Satan is silenced, to be powerless. Small wonder that Isaac can have the temerity to lay our shortcomings at God's door.

Now this rosy view of Israel's essential blamelessness is clearly contestable. It is only God Who is willing to grant it credence. The hard-headed Satan refuses to countenance it. It is only on Yom Kippur when he is, so to speak, muzzled, that it has a short-lived viability.

What is God's point of view, and what is the Satan's?

❀ ❀ ❀

Our quest takes us back to the *Bris bein HaBesarim* when God first promised *Eretz Yisrael* to Abraham and his descendants. Abraham asked, "*HASHEM God, by what may I know that I will indeed inherit it.*" The Sages sum up God's answer in two words, בִּזְכוּת הַקָּרְבָּנוֹת the sacrificial service will guarantee it.

What was Abraham's question and what did God answer?

Maharal understands the conversation as follows: Abraham certainly believed that he would be given the Land. But, he wondered, would he be able to keep it? What if his children sinned? Is it not conceivable that all his vast spiritual capital would be squandered by descendants who would care nothing for his passion, who would chip away and ultimately erode all that he had won with so much struggle?

God's answer was that this would not, and indeed could not, happen. Abraham's children would always possess an irreducible core of sanctity which would be impervious to the ravages of sin. Where the other nations, with dreary and dispiriting predictability, commit self-destruction and disappear from the stage of history, Israel is different. The evil which others perpetrate is a cancer which gnaws away at their vitals and consumes them — utterly. Our sins, terrible as they are, will disfigure and besmirch us horribly — but will leave our essence untouched.

This is the meaning of בִּזְכוּת הַקָּרְבָּנוֹת. Reference is, in the first place to the atoning חַטָּאת sacrifice which only Abraham's children possess. The root חטא from which חַטָּאת is formed has the base meaning, *to cleanse*. The act of cleansing is possible only when the filth is no more than surface deep. While the perfidy of rebellion may demand punishment the stain of sin can never leave an indelible mark on the Jewish soul.

Clearly, there is a point to which evil cannot penetrate.

This is the secret of eternal Israel as revealed to Abraham.

What does this really mean? Wherein does our difference lie? What are the implications of our choseness?

כל נדרי — *Kol Nidrei*

Bil'am recognized us as a nation apart — עַם לְבָדָד. We are a lonesome people. *Psalms* 145 [. . . אַשְׁרֵי] which is an acrostic based upon the *aleph-bais* skips the letter נ because it hints at נְפִילָה, *falling*. We are prone to fall because alone among the nations we have no one to support us. We can look only to God — because it is God who helps all who fall — סוֹמֵךְ ה׳ לְכָל הַנּוֹפְלִים (*Berachos* 4b).

The nations help one another — but they do not help us. We are the eternal stranger with whom no one quite knows what to do. When they do not kill us, they circle us warily; distrustful, threatened and grudging. In the battle which Jacob and Esau fought even before they were born, Esau was granted this world — we, the other. For the nations, "here" is where home is — for us "here" is a פְּרוֹזְדוֹר, *an ante-chamber* which, at the very best, offers a meaningless and impersonal comfort, to be tolerated while God wills us to be here. But it touches our reality not at all.

We live, then, a dual existence. We are in this world but are not of it; are subject to its vicissitudes but are not — at our essence — touched by them. Its blandishments attract us, we are subject to the *Yetzer Hara* who is indigenous to it; are prone, so very prone, to the sloth, the animal cravings, the dreadful pride, the pitiful smallness which are the dark side of its physicality — but all these touch only that part of us which is "here".

We become blackened by sin like the sun-drenched *tents of Kedar*. But the discoloration is superficial — never essential. A cleansing חַטָאת, a soul-shattering *teshuvah*, will quickly reveal the shining white of *Solomon's curtains* which lies beneath.

※ ※ ※

Our attempt to understand God's perspective upon Israel's sins — the perspective which has viability only on Yom Kippur when the Satan is silenced — must now lead us to a closer analysis of the precise nature of Yom Kippur as a day of atonement.

Yom Kippur received its unique character in the first year of our desert wanderings. It was on that day that God gave Moses the second tablets — granting Israel final forgiveness for the sin of the Golden Calf.

> ... [Moses] came down on the tenth [of Tishrei] and found Israel engaged in fasting and prayer. It was on that day that Moses was told, סָלַחְתִּי כִּדְבָרֶיךָ, and God marked it as a day of forgiveness and pardon for all generations ... (*Tanchuma, Ki Sisa* 31).

There seems little doubt that our custom to end the pre-*maariv* section on *Kol Nidrei* night with, סְלַח נָא ... וַיֹּאמֶר ה׳ סָלַחְתִּי כִּדְבָרֶיךָ, derives from this *midrash*. However, this does not relieve us from the need to examine the claim of the *midrash* that the words, סָלַחְתִּי כִּדְבָרֶיךָ were uttered on that first Yom Kippur. For, in the Torah, they occur in *Numbers* 14:20, after Moses had interceded for the people who had sinned in the matter of the *Meraglim*. They do not, at all, appear in connection with the sin of the Golden Calf.

How then, do we deal with the midrash? And, with what justification do we assign such a central role to these words, which, as the Torah tells it, seem to have no connection at all with Yom Kippur?

To gain a better understanding, we should first analyze the precise meaning of the phrase. What did God mean when He said, סָלַחְתִּי כִּדְבָרֶיךָ, *I have forgiven in accordance with your words*. What *words* are those?

Rashi writes: Because of what you said, "*Lest they say that it is because HASHEM is unable ...*"

Thus, the *words* of Moses to which God acceded were his argument that if God were to kill out the Israelites in the wilderness it would cause a *chilul hashem* among the gentile nations who would conclude that God had simply been unable to fulfill the promises which He had made to His people.

Now *Rashi*'s comment requires analysis. A careful reading of Moses' speech — to which God answered, סָלַחְתִּי כִּדְבָרֶיךָ — shows that it consists of two parts. The first is the argument of the potential *chilul hashem* of which we spoke above, the second is a prayer for God's mercy.

The words, סָלַחְתִּי כִּדְבָרֶיךָ follow hard upon the second part — that is the prayer for mercy — and we would have supposed that *Rashi* might have interpreted, כִּדְבָרֶיךָ as meaning; in answer to your prayer. *Rashi* does not do so and, instead, he has it refer specifically to the argument part of the speech.

Commentators offer various explanations for *Rashi*'s decision to choose the one over the other. These are text-based. Thus, for example, *Sefer Zikaron* offers two possible justifications. The first is that if the prayer had been meant, the word כִּדְבָרֶיךָ would have been superfluous. God could simply have said, סָלַחְתִּי , and the meaning would have been self-explanatory. The second, that: It is not seemly that a master say to his student, "I have done in accordance with your words." Rather, the meaning is that your words [that is your arguments] have convinced Me [and I am acting upon them because of My conviction, not because you have directed Me.]

Be the textual evidence what it may, we must still ask ourselves why it was the force of Moses' argument — but not his prayer — which moved God to forgive.

The answer must surely be that the transgression had been such a heinous one that forgiveness in their own merit was out of the question. [Note that Moses in his prayer does not invoke the merit of the Patriarchs — see *Ramban*, there]. It was only Moses's appeal to the need to avoid the terrible *chillul hashem* which would result from the destruction of His people which was able to, so to speak, sway God.

We have already explored the potency of that argument in an earlier essay [*Perhaps He Will Look Upon Us As Servants*] and quoted the *Ramban* upon which it is based. Because of the extreme significance of his insights for our thesis here, we quote him once more, in full:

> [The statement [at *Deuteronomy* 32:26] that God had wanted to destroy us refers to our present exile ... in which, if absolute justice were to hold sway, we would have to remain forever, were it not for the fury of the foe. This indicates that in our present situation there is nothing left of the merit of the fathers [תַּמָּה זְכוּת אָבוֹת] and we can hope for salvation only in the merit of God's great name. This is in accordance with the numerous passages in the prophets in which it is stated clearly that God will help us in our exile not because we deserve it but only to avoid the desecration of His name. It is for this reason that Moses, in his prayer, said: *"Then the nations which have heard of Your fame might say ... "* And God agreed with this argument and answered: *'I have decided to forgive in accordance with that which you have said* [סָלַחְתִּי כִּדְבָרֶיךָ]*."*
>
> Now the sense of this phrase is by no means that it expresses a desire to flaunt His strength to His enemies, for all the people are as nothing to Him, they are utterly worthless in His eyes. But [God's consideration was based on the fact that] He had created a physical world so that humans might recognize Him and adore Him. But — He granted them absolute freedom. They may choose to do either good or evil. Now when mankind chose freely to sin and to deny Him, only this one nation [Israel] remained true to Him. Through the miracles which accompanied them throughout their history, He made it known that He is the One Omnipotent God — and this became known to all the nations.
>
> Now if God should ever decide to destroy them, then all the nations would forget all these miracles and

no one would ever mention them again. And even if they would occasionally come to mind, people would ascribe all these occurrences to natural causes with no current significance. Thus would the entire purpose of creation be undermined for no one would remember God meaningfully, but on the contrary, people would only anger Him.

Therefore the very will which prompted God to create the world in the first place, must guarantee that Israel remain His people eternally. For it is they alone, among all the nations, who are close to Him and who have an accurate perception of Him.

Now that is the meaning of the verse, *When HASHEM will judge His people, He will look mercifully upon His servants* (there v.36). The meaning is that God will, in His mercy, recall that they are His servants who remained true to Him throughout their exile, loyally bearing the burdens of suffering and slavery ...

This, then, is the meaning of סָלַחְתִּי כִּדְבָרֶיךָ. The phrase speaks of a symbiosis between God and His people. A relationship of mutual love and, as it were, dependence, which makes the disappearance of Israel from the stage of history unthinkable.

We can now return to the first Yom Kippur, the day when Moses was given the second tablets, and the assertion of the midrash that it was then that God had said, סָלַחְתִּי כִּדְבָרֶיךָ.

We know for certain what the *midrash* does not mean. Clearly, the phrase was not said at that occasion. The meaning can only be that God's forgiveness of the sin of the Golden Calf gave tangible expression to the principle [כִּדְבָרֶיךָ] which was enunciated only much later.

That principle is the truly shattering assertion of the *Ramban* that, *the very will which prompted God to create the world in the first place, must guarantee that Israel remain His people eternally. For it is they alone, among all the nations, who are close to Him and who have an accurate perception of Him.*

Indeed, God had defined the sin of the golden Calf as a national, not an individual, straying: *Go down for your people have acted destructively . . . (Exodus 32:7 ff.).* Moses, too, prayed on behalf of the people — *Why HASHEM should Your anger be kindled against Your nation . . . (v. 11 ff.)* — and not on behalf of individual sinners. It stands to reason that that which motivated God to forgive was a rationale which had *Klal Yisrael* as its focus.

And, indeed, the atonement function of Yom Kippur appears to address the community rather than the individual. It is only thus that we can understand that the *Sa'ir HaMishtaleach* can elicit atonement for certain levels of transgressions even without *teshuvah* of the individual [see *Rambam, Teshuvah* 1:3]. Clearly the *Sa'ir*, a communal sacrifice, atones for its owners — the community — and everyone who has not read himself out of membership in that community partakes of its cleansing force.

That first Yom Kippur, then, was the day upon which, once and for all, God confirmed His interdependent relationship as it were, in the sense that *Ramban* has explained it, with Israel. The faculty that, . . . *they are His servants who remained true to Him throughout their exile, loyally bearing the burdens of suffering and slavery . . .* , is grounded in, and nurtured by, Israel's essential other-worldliness, the hard core of absolute sanctity which can never be eroded.

And therefore, Yom Kippur was set aside as that day among all others upon which that uniqueness would be celebrated. Essence is not form and it can never be the only defining factor. We *do* live in this world, we *are*, at an external level, subject to its siren songs. That reality is the Satan's sphere of influence and — as is his duty — he will not tolerate an appeal to essential goodness when all-too-real violations of this-worldly norms must be punished. Throughout the year a claim that we were coerced into sinning by a malevolent *Yetzer Hara* from without, will help us not at all. But Yom Kippur is different. The sheer power of that pure light of truth which first infused a pallid, uninspiring, temporal reality with intimations of eternity, when a yet-to-be-uttered סָלַחְתִּי כִּדְבָרֶיךָ first impacted upon history, effectively silences the Satan on that day.

Yom Kippur is the celebration of a truth beneath the truth. It is the day upon which God, as it were, allows Himself to see us as we really are.

And so, it is eminently appropriate that, even before we begin the actual *Maariv* service we set the tone for the day by beginning with the ... וְנִסְלַח verse and lead from it into סְלַח נָא ... and from there to the all important, סָלַחְתִּי כִּדְבָרֶיךָ. As we have now learned, these verses, taken together, define the day in its essential features.

※ ※ ※

At the beginning of this essay we set ourselves two tasks. We wanted to understand the וְנִסְלַח passage, up to and including סָלַחְתִּי כִּדְבָרֶיךָ in its own terms, and then to place it in the larger framework of the entire pre-*Maariv* section.

Accordingly, we will now move to the beginning of this section.

The formal start of the Yom Kippur service is the עַל דַּעַת הַמָּקוֹם ... in which we announce that, for this day only, we will welcome the עֲבַרְיָנִים, the *transgressors*, to pray with us in the synagogue.

The background for this proclamation is as follows. There was a time when bans [נִדּוּי] were pronounced against people who flouted communal edicts or otherwise acted in ways which were inimical to communal standards. People against whom these ban had been instituted could not be counted in a *minyan*, and, where warranted, could even be forbidden access to the synagogue (*Orech Chaim* 55:12).

On Yom Kippur we lift any such interdictions for the day.

At first blush we would assume that this is a simple human gesture towards these unfortunates. It is simply too harsh to exclude them from communal prayer on Yom Kippur.

But, this is not the case. It transpires that we invite these transgressors to pray with us, not for their benefit but for our's.

As a source for our usage, *Gra* adduces *Kerisos* 6b where R' Shimon Chasida taught: No communal fast in which sinners [פּוֹשְׁעֵי יִשְׂרָאֵל] are not involved, is worthy of its name. Witness the *chelbenah* which had a foul smell and is still listed among the ingredients of the *incense*.

Now, surely, the *chelbenah* was included in the *ketores*, not for its own sake but because it somehow contributed to the savor of the aroma.

R' Shimon Chasida is teaching that even the wicked — foul smelling as they surely are — have something to contribute to the communal wholesomeness.

This truth is borne out by *Menachos* 27a: Of the four *kinds* involved with the *mitzvah* of Lulav, two of them [the esrog and the palm tree] bear fruits and two [the myrtle and the willow] do not. The two which are fruitful cannot dispense with the two which are not; the two which are not fruitful cannot dispense with the two which are. No one can fulfill his obligation unless they are all involved. So too is it with Israel בהרצאה [When they fast. It is required that all of them be part of one grouping — the righteous and the wicked ... (*Rashi*)]

Again the strange formulation. What possible benefit can the righteous among us draw from the presence of the wicked?

We suspect that the solution may be as follows: When we see a person who is righteous, we know something about him as a person. We can intuit the inner battles which he has fought, the iron discipline with which he has learned to bend his will, we can guess at the prayers and the tears which were the road-markers of his arduous journey. In short he is defined — as a person — by the aura of his accomplishments.

But, we know nothing yet about his people.

The רָשָׁע is different. As an individual he is foul-smelling and disgusting. But — *even the most shallow of them are as full of mitzvos as a pomegranate is full of pits* (*Berachos* 57a). That even the least worthy among us has an indestructible core of sanctity, that none of us are ever wholly bad — that tells us something about what *Klal Yisroel* is. It is that insight beyond all others which, as we stand fasting before our God, will stand us in good stead.

The עֲבַרְיָנִים may need us — but our need of them is even greater.

We have learned that the this pre-*Maariv* section ends — through the . . . וְנִסְלַח passage — on a note of celebration of the inner sanctity of *Klal Yisrael*. We have now learned that this is also the theme of the opening, . . . עַל דַּעַת הַמָּקוֹם passage.

※ ※ ※

We now move to the main *Kol Nidrei* passage. How did this proclamation, which is, after all only a formal pronouncement annulling vows which will be made during the coming year, win such pride of place in the Yom Kippur service.

Here we must turn to another of the great themes which give Yom Kippur its meaning. Yom Kippur is a day permeated by the concept of חֵרוּת, *freedom*.

We begin our analysis with the well-known *midrash* on *Psalms* 27:1: . . . לְדָוִד ה׳ אוֹרִי וְיִשְׁעִי אוֹרִי refers to Rosh Hashanah when we experience God as *light*; יִשְׁעִי hints at Yom Kippur when we experience Him as *salvation* (*Vayikra Rabba* 21).

In the context of our discussion, it is the second of these interpretations to which we must direct our attention.

If we require *salvation* that can only be because we are captive to a malevolent force from which we need to be freed.

For understanding, we turn to the custom of sounding the shofar at the end of the *Ne'ilah* service. *Tur* 624 believes that this shofar blast hints at the shofar which was blown on Yom Kippur during the *Yovel* year.[3]

Commentators question *Tur's* reasoning. Why, they wonder, should we need to commemorate the *Yovel* blasts on every ordinary Yom Kippur? If *Tur's* reasoning is correct we should sound the shofar only once in fifty years when the *Yovel* would normally come out? Accordingly they offer different explanations for the custom.

To understand the *Tur* we turn to *Maharal*, in his *Drush LeShabbos Teshuvah*. Because of the profound significance of this passage, we quote it in full.

> ... for Yom Kippur is a day of personal salvation. For when a person sins, the sin enslaves him and on Yom Kippur he is freed from this sin. That is the thought behind the shofar blast on the night when Yom Kippur ends. For a shofar blast hints at being freed as did the shofar of the Yom Kippur of the *Yovel*.

The *Tur*, then, does not mean that the shofar blast simply recalls the fact that a shofar was also blown during the *Yovel*. Rather he views the shofar blast at *Neilah* in the same category as the *Yovel* blast. It is the sound of freedom and it announces our emancipation from the dreadful mastery of sin.

---

3. The background to *Tur's* explanation is as follows.

The shofar is to be sounded on the Yom Kippur of the *Yovel* year in precisely the same form as it is usually sounded on Rosh Hashanah (Mishnah, *Rosh Hashanah* 26b). This, because the Rosh Hashanah of *Yovel*, that is, the day from which its sanctity as expressed in the freeing of slaves and the returning of real property to its original owners, begins, is the tenth of Tishrei rather than the first.

Rashi, there, points out that the congruence between the laws of sounding the shofar on Yom Kippur of the *Yovel* and on a normal Rosh Hashanah does not derive from a similarity of function. On Rosh Hashanah the shofar belongs in the context of תְּפִלָּה and זִכָּרוֹן while on the Yom Kippur of the *Yovel* it simply announces the freeing of the slaves and the return of the real property.

Yom Kippur is יִשְׁעִי, the day of *salvation* from the filth in which the sins which we committed throughout the year, encrusted us.

※ ※ ※

Now to the actual *Kol Nidrei* passage.

Why do we pronounce an annulment of next years vows on Yom Kippur?

Commentators adduce *Nedarim* 23b: He who wishes that the vows which he will make throughout the year should have no validity, let him stand up on Rosh Hashanah and declare, "All vows which I shall make should be annulled!"

Without, in the present context, entering into a general discussion of the ability to annul vows before they are made, and why there should be an allowance for making such a proclamation at the beginning of the year, we do need to ask ourselves why, in view of the fact that the Gemara suggests that this should be done on Rosh Hashanah, do we proclaim it on Yom Kippur?

Rosh asks this question and suggests two possible answers. First: Synagogues tend to be fuller on Yom Kippur and thus more people can benefit from the proclamation. Second: Yom Kippur too is called Rosh Hashanah — in the context of the *Yovel*.

Gra brings only the second answer.

But, that seems to leave the problem unsolved. Granted that Yom Kippur is called Rosh Hashanah, but Rosh Hashanah is certainly called Rosh Hashanah. Why then change the proclamation to Yom Kippur?

We may perhaps surmise as follows.

The fact that a synonym for נֶדֶר is אִסָּר from אָסַר, *to bind*, and that, moreover, the expression favored by the Sages for the judicial annulment of a vow — הַתָּרַת נְדָרִים, means literally, *the untying* of the נֶדֶר, certainly suggest that the Torah looks upon the נֶדֶר as a binding. *Nedarim* make us unfree.

Let us analyze this a little further.

God filled His world with beauty and goodness, not that we should deny ourselves these pleasures but that we might savor them and delight in them. The Torah, *Kiddushin* 30b teaches us, is a prophylactic which, when used "as prescribed" opens up a world of legitimate enjoyment to us: [אֶת דְּבָרַי אֵלֶּה] וְשַׂמְתֶּם is to be read as, [וְ]סַם תָּם, *a perfect healing device*: We might compare His giving us His Torah, to a man who wounded his son terribly and then placed some healing ointment on the wound. He said, "My son! As long as this healing ointment is on your wound, you may eat, drink and bathe in hot or cold water as much as you want. You have nothing at all to fear. But remove it — and your wound will fester."

Our love of indulgence in this-worldly pleasures is a terrible wound. Unchecked, it will fester and ultimately destroy us. Subordinated to the Torah's stern but loving discipline, these cravings have a legitimate function and open up a world of delight — which, it is God's wish, that we should savor.[4]

The *nazir*, the ascetic who vows, among other things, not to drink wine, is a sinner. He has inflicted an unwarranted and therefore unjustified denial upon himself. Wine was created to *gladden men's heart*. Who are we to invent prohibitions beyond those which the Torah imposed! (*Nazir* 19a)

Nedarim are normally undertaken to help in disciplining the unruly cravings which so often refuse to leave us any peace. They curb our desires — but the price we pay is that they inhibit our freedom of action. They lend their strength to our weakness, their

---

4. It goes without saying that פְּרִישׁוּת, the voluntary abstention from certain physical pleasures, has a place, and a very significant one, in our moral training. But that is always as an educational and disciplining *tool*. It is generally not an objective end in itself.

It is also conceivable that a person would be of such spiritual stature that he finds no pleasure in, or need for, physical fulfillment beyond the most basic levels [see *Mesilas Yesharim* on *Perishus*]. Certainly such a person would not be called upon to savor pleasures for which he has no taste.

barriers to our desires. They are useful — but sinful (*Nedarim* 22a). They frustrate God's wishes for us. They deny us the legitimate enjoyment of pleasures which it is His pleasure that we should taste.

This insight — we suggest— can help us to understand the place which the *Kol Nidrei* passage has in the pre-*Maariv* section of the Yom Kippur service.

We saw above that the underlying theme of the day is חֵרוּת, freedom from the encrusted evil which so often holds us in thrall. Because of this, we begin the day by asserting our determination to be and to remain free. We are determined to look to God, and only to Him, for guidance in what is and what is not desirable for us. We proclaim now, that if, in the coming year, we experience a moment of weakness and feel the need to encumber ourselves with the chains which our fallibility forges, that those chains shall be broken. Later, when the time comes, we may have to change our minds. But for now, as we are about to enter into the awesome sanctity of this day of days, we declare our identification with its aims.

The *Kol Nidrei* section fits smoothly between the opening, עַל דַּעַת הַמָּקוֹם ... and the closing, ... וְנִסְלַח passages. These; as we have seen, celebrated the indestructible core of sanctity which defines the essential nature of *Klal Yisrael*. *Kol Nidrei*, in proclaiming ourselves as free before God is part of that message. בִּלְתִּי לַה׳ לְבַדּוֹ! As we are about to envelope ourselves in the sanctity of the day, we sharpen our focus both inward and outward. HASHEM is our God, we are His people — and in the symbiosis that binds Him to us and us to Him lies our certainty that we shall emerge from this awesome day — cleansed.

שֶׁאֵין אָנוּ עַזֵּי פָנִים ... ❧
For We Are Not Brazen Faced ...

Now, after the Temple has been destroyed, when we no longer have an altar to effect our atonement, there is only *teshuvah* ... (*Rambam Teshuvah* 1:3).

The central theme of our Yom Kippur is *teshuvah*. And *viduy* is a necessary part of the *teshuvah* process [see *Rambam, Teshuvah* 2:2].

A short, and necessarily incomplete, survey of opinions concerning the obligation to do *teshuvah* on Yom Kippur is in order.

> *Rabbeinu Yonah* in *Shaarey Teshuvah* 2:5 states unequivocally that: There is an obligation mandated by the Torah [מִצְוַת עֲשֵׂה מִן הַתּוֹרָה] that each of us inspire himself to do *teshuvah* on Yom Kippur ...
>
> *Rambam* is less clear. At *Teshuvah* 2:7 he writes: Yom Kippur is a time of *teshuvah* for all — for the individual as well as for the community. It is the ultimate point of forgiveness for Israel [קֵץ מְחִילָה וּסְלִיחָה לְיִשְׂרָאֵל]. For this reason all are obliged to do *teshuvah* and to make confession [וִדּוּי] on Yom Kippur ...
>
> *Rambam* is absolutely clear in stating that we are to do *teshuvah*, without, however, stating in so many words that it is a מִצְוַת עֲשֵׂה מִן הַתּוֹרָה, as does *Rabbeinu Yonah*. He certainly does not count the obligation to do *teshuvah* on Yom Kippur in his *Sefer HaMitzvos*.
>
> It seems likely that his perception of the obligation is more in line with that of the *Shulchan Aruch HaRav* who writes that the obligation to do *teshuvah* does not inhere in the day as, for example, the obligation to eat *matzah* on

Pesach. Rather it is akin to the requirement that anyone who brings a sacrifice is obliged to do *teshuvah* in conjunction with this act of Divine service. The sense is that, if God, so to speak, declares Himself ready to offer us atonement, it is our obligation to react to this willingness by doing all that is in our power to further God's will. We do *teshuvah* so that we might indeed merit the cleansing which God is willing to perform.

So too on Yom Kippur. It is a day on which God promises to atone our sins and to cleanse us — כִּי בַיּוֹם הַזֶּה יְכַפֵּר עֲלֵיכֶם לְטַהֵר אֶתְכֶם ... — and that, in itself, without a specific command, obliges us to do *teshuvah*.

If this is indeed the case it would serve as the key to understanding *Chayei Adam* who writes in *Klal* 142 that *teshuvah* is to be undertaken *before* Yom Kippur. We suspect that according to *Rabbeinu Yonah's* formulation this would be impossible. It would be the equivalent of eating *matzah* before Pesach — something that is manifestly ridiculous. If, however, it is not an obligation vested in the *day* but in the *event* — then such a position is unsurprising.

This understanding of the obligation to do *teshuvah* might also underlie the custom to say *viduy* during the minchah service on Erev Yom Kippur. We do this out of fear that we might become incapacitated before Yom Kippur begins. This custom would also make little sense if the obligation to do *teshuvah* would reside in the day in the same sense that the obligation to eat *matzah* relates to Pesach.

The wording of our passage is strange: *For we are not brazen-faced or stiff-necked that we would say before You, . . . "We have not sinned." But, surely we have sinned.*

We are about to recite the אָשַׁמְנוּ confession. With each letter of the *aleph-bet* we admit to having sinned in any number of ways.

Why preface this with the self-evident statement that we are not brazen-faced enough to deny our guilt? Does our recitation of אָשַׁמְנוּ not make this obvious?

Would we, for example, introduce our daily recitation of the שְׁמַע with the statement that we are not the kind of people who refuse to accept the *yoke of God's kingship*? Surely not. We are saying the שְׁמַע and that fact speaks for itself. Why not let our *viduy* itself testify that we do not say, "We have not sinned"?

❧ ❧ ❧

What precisely is *viduy*?

Viduy occurs in the Torah only as a verb deriving from the root ידה. Besides the concept of *confession* this root serves also to express, *casting down* [וַיַּדּוּ אֶבֶן בִּי . . .], and *praising* or *thanking* — concepts which are so close to one another that it is difficult to know precisely when the one is meant, and when the other.

It is striking that the Torah invariably uses the *hisp'ael*, the reflexive form [הִתְוַדָּה], to express the sense, *to confess*. The reason for this cannot be that the *kal* form cannot carry this connotation, because we do find it used in this sense in *Psalms* 32:5 [. . . וּמוֹדֶה וְעֹזֵב יְרֻחָם] and in *Proverbs* 28:13 [אוֹדֶה עֲלֵי פְשָׁעַי].

How, then are we to understand the unwavering and thus, principled, use of the *hispa'el*?

We can understand this best by considering the apparent versatility of the ידה root. What do, *casting down*, *praising*, *thanking*, and *confession* have in common?

If we take the base-meaning of the root as, *to cast down*, the other uses follow readily. They all involve a degree of self-abnegation, of *casting oneself down* before another. Each is an action which derives from an awareness of one's own deficiency in the face of another's supremacy. We *praise* people for qualities which we find admirable and which we miss in ourselves. We *thank* them for favors dispensed for which we were dependent upon them. And we confess to inadequacies in the fulfillment of diverse legitimate claims upon us.

Certainly מוֹדֶה, in the *kal* could serve to describe the act of confession as readily as it can take on the meaning, to praise or to thank. But, it would not, in that voice, do justice to the full implication of what the act of *viduy* before God requires. *Viduy* is to be much more than a simple admission. It must entail a gut-wrenching inner dislocation, a ruthless probing that plays havoc with the veneer of big and little frauds which, in ordinary circumstances, we use so efficiently to allay our conscience. It must lay bare the innermost recesses of our being to the harsh and unforgiving light of truth, it must leave us shattered and broken by the sheer enormity of the lie we have been living.

We do not simply *cast ourselves down* before God [מוֹדֶה]. We undergo a metamorphosis. We become nothing more than deflated relics of our wicked bombast. We have nothing left but our — *prostration*. We define ourselves by its terms, know no truth besides our fall. There is nothing left to us but that we are a mass of collapsed potentialities, the sorry remnants of high hopes gone sour [מִתְוַדֶה].

Let us take our analysis a little further.

In the *Kohen Gadol's viduy* which is part of the *avodah* which we say during *Mussaf*, the actual wording —חָטָאתִי עָוִיתִי פָּשַׁעְתִּי ... and so on — is preceded by the words, אָנָּא הַשֵּׁם. This formulation is based on *Yoma* 37a which derives the obligation to use the introductory אָנָּא from Moses's confession on the occasion of the sin of the Golden Calf: ... אָנָּא חָטָא הָעָם הַזֶּה חֲטָאָה גְדוֹלָה.

Rambam, Teshuvah 1:1 broadens this requirement to include even the *viduy* of individuals, and *Shaarei Teshuvah* to *Orech Chaim* 131:1 rules accordingly. Some *machzorim* include the word in the individual *viduy* [... אָנָּא תָבֹא לְפָנֶיךָ תְּפִלָּתֵינוּ], others do not.

What, precisely, does the word, אָנָּא, mean?

Interestingly, it displays the same versatility which we discovered earlier for the root, ידה. It is *Ibn Ezra* who points out that the אָנָּא used by Moses (*Exodus* 32:31) is related to the אָנָה [although with a final ה instead of an א] of *Psalms* 116:16 [אָנָּה ה' ... כִּי אֲנִי עַבְדֶּךָ]. In the *Exodus* passage it carries the connotation of *confession* [... פִּיּוּס אוֹ דֶּרֶךְ הוֹדָאָה], while in *Psalms* it is an expression of *gratitude* or *praise*.

We can dig a little further.

Radak in *Sefer HaShorashim* lists the word as an expansion of אָן.

אָן itself has a variety of connotations: It is used as an interrogative of *place* — אָנָה אֲנַחְנוּ עוֹלִים ... (*Deuteronomy* 1:28), and of *time* — עַד אָנָה יְנַאֲצֻנִי הָעָם הַזֶּה ... (*Numbers* 14:11). It is also the form from which the personal pronoun, אֲנִי, *I*, is built.

We suspect that the root concept, אן, is structured to accord with its inner meaning. The letter א, connotes the number, *one*, that is, *the singular state*. נ is the letter which denotes *solitariness*, the sense of being quite alone because all the others have a pair to equal ten but נ can be only added to itself to equal ten. [See under *The Entire Family of Israel Shall be Forgiven*]. Thus, the addition of the נ to the א — אן — turns it from the possible *first* of a series into a singular *one* which connects with no one at all — which stands alone.

Alone, means without any supportive framework. I do not know where to go — I ask, לְאָן. I do not know, how long — I ask, עַד אָנָא. I speak of myself, unattached and unique — and I say, אֲנִי. [The נִי ... ending probably derives from the first person suffix in the past tense and is thus appropriate for the personal pronoun, *I*.]

And from there, to the concept of *viduy*. Not only am I מִתְוַדֶּה rather than מוֹדֶה, but I also preface my confession with אָנָּא. I am alone, disoriented, bewildered. I have lost my spiritual bearings. I am desperate to find support in the only source which is available to me — in God — but I know myself to be unworthy. I pour out my heart in *viduy* — and begin to feel that I am alone no longer.

❦ ❦ ❦

The prophet Yechezkel talks of a time when God will, *remove the stony heart* [לֵב הָאֶבֶן] *from their flesh and give them a heart of flesh* [לֵב בָּשָׂר] (Ezekiel 11:19). בָּשָׂר, *flesh*, derives from the root, בשר, *to announce*. It is the means by which *messages concerning* tactility, temperature and so on are conveyed to the brain (*Hirsch*). Thus the לֵב בָּשָׂר is the sensitive heart which has not been petrified into the rock-like obtuseness which is dead to all feeling — the לֵב הָאֶבֶן.

Succah 52a speaks of seven names by which the *Yetzer Hara* is called. The most terrible of all seems to be אֶבֶן, *the stone* — inanimate, insensitive, closed off in a dreadful solitude to which nothing at all can penetrate.[1]

Such a לֵב הָאֶבֶן is impervious to the feelings of dislocation which we described above. These require an honest, open heart which is ready to admit to the dreadful havoc that sin brings in our lives and, concomitantly, to the sense of urgency that profound changes must be made — feelings which undergird our ability to stand before God pouring out the litany of our wrongdoing.

This is the key to everything — the *ability to admit*.

In the final moments before the catastrophic destruction of the first Temple, Jeremiah called out to the people, *See My quarrel with you comes about — because you say, "I have not sinned!"* (Jeremiah 2:35). There might yet have been hope. Israel's sins, dreadful as they were, might yet have been eradicated by a sincere repentance. Their fate was sealed because of their obduracy (*Yalkut*, there). When we admit nothing we learn nothing. The prophet's despair is palpable: *You displayed the arrogant smirk of*

---

1. In fact, אֶבֶן is the sixth, not the seventh, on the list, which seems to belie the statement that it is the most terrible of all. However the seventh, and therefore apparently the worst, is צְפוּנִי, *the hidden one*. This is not a description of qualitative evil, as are the other six, but of a state in which the *Yetzer HaRa* is no more recognizable as a separate entity, but has fused utterly into the personality thus establishing an *identity* with evil. Accordingly we seem to be correct in asserting that in the actual hierarchy of evil, אֶבֶן is indeed the worst.

the harlot — you simply refused to feel any shame (see Jeremiah 3:3).

What is the source of this inability to acknowledge guilt?

Our passage makes clear that it is a function of עַזּוּת פָּנִים, *brazenness*. שֶׁאֵין אָנוּ עַזֵּי פָנִים ... לוֹמַר לְפָנֶיךָ ... צַדִּיקִים אֲנַחְנוּ וְלֹא חָטָאנוּ. An עַז פָּנִים would say, לֹא חָטָאתִי.

The *midrash* to the *Jeremiah* verse which we quoted above (3:3) ponders the nature of עַזּוּת פָּנִים: Whoever is brazen-faced ... has certainly already sinned ...

How so?

The *midrash* to *Koheles* 8:1: וְעֹז פָּנָיו יְשֻׁנֶּא ..., finds that the paradigmatic עַז פָּנִים is Adam — when he sought to lay the blame for his transgression upon his wife, or perhaps, upon God Himself: הָאִשָּׁה אֲשֶׁר נָתַתָּה עִמָּדִי הִיא נָתְנָה לִי מִן הָעֵץ וָאֹכֵל, *The woman whom You placed with me — she gave me from the tree, and I ate.*

We are עַזֵּי פָנִים when we refuse to shoulder responsibility for our actions, when rather than face the heinousness of our wrongdoing we block the passages to our hearts. עַזּוּת is the brazen deadening of sensibility to the feelings of guilt and alienation which, if we would but let them, might be the key to our rehabilitation. The עַז פָּנִים has petrified his heart. His is the לֵב הָאֶבֶן which rock-like is impervious to the entreaties of his conscience. *Viduy* can have no meaning for him at all.

Such a one may well mouth the word חָטָאנוּ, but really, in his heart, be saying, צַדִּיקִים אֲנַחְנוּ וְלֹא חָטָאנוּ. Not his, the broken and submissive spirit, the havoc and the hope, the vulnerability and the iron determination, the prayer and the sobbing — above all, not his, the truth brooking no shadings of ambiguity, which *viduy* entails.

❈ ❈ ❈

Among the long litany of transgressions of which we speak in the עַל חֵטְא section of the *viduy*, we have, וִדּוּי פֶּה, the sin of *insincere confession*. My Rosh HaYeshivah, the *gaon*, HaRav

Aharon Kotler זצ״ל explained the heinousness of this particular fault: The very act of *viduy*, the standing before God listing sin upon sin which we have committed, must itself be construed as *legse majestea* of the highest order. How can we have the gall to tell the King of Kings that His word meant nothing to us at all, that we went upon our untroubled way, inattentive to His wishes and commands? If saying לֹא חָטָאתִי requires עַזּוּת פָּנִים, can it not be argued that saying חָטָאתִי is even worse?

And, yet, God bids us to be מִתְוַדֶּה before Him.

This can only be understood as an unbounded act of loving-kindness. God knows that the *ba'al teshuvah* needs the catharsis which *viduy* provides. He needs to pour out his grief, his guilt, his terrors and his hopes, needs to feel the dreadful shame of admitting — mostly to himself — the abject failure which he has made of his life. He needs, if he is to begin the long and difficult way home, to confront the blighted potential, the wasted hopes, the sorrow and pity of his petty stupidity.

And so God tells us to be מִתְוַדֶּה. He is willing to overlook the dreadful insult to His majesty — so that we can become *baalei teshuvah*.

What, then, if we abuse this gift, if we do not summon the shame and the contrition which *viduy* demands? Would this not be the most dreadful violation of trust? Would not our אָשַׁמְנוּ, our בָּגַדְנוּ, our גָּזַלְנוּ become barbs of disdain hurled at a loving Father Whose hand is even now stretched out to us, hopeful — oh so hopeful — that we might understand? Each new sin added to the list, each letter in the *aleph-bet* marshalled to lend form and structure to this caricature of a confession, would only be another affirmation of our refusal to bow, another assertion that, in Jeremiah's words, וַתַּעֲשִׂי הָרָעוֹת וַתּוּכָל, we are masters of our fate, that we can do evil — and that no one can or will stop us (Jeremiah 3:5).

If we say the שְׁמַע without the requisite *kavanah* we have missed an opportunity, have not fulfilled an obligation. If we are

מִתְוַדֶה without the requisite *kavanah* we have committed the most dreadful חִלוּל ה'.

Before we dare to take on the daunting challenge of *viduy* we, as it were, ask God's permission to approach. We are not, so we say to Him, עַזֵּי פָנִים who will abuse the privilege which has been granted us: אֲבָל אֲנַחְנוּ חָטָאנוּ! The awareness of sin defines, for this moment at the very least, our being and our consciousness. Our mind is closed to any other thought than that our lives are an absolute shambles. We have totally missed the mark to which our lives were aimed [thus חֵטְא from חטא, *to miss the mark*]. This is our truth, this our broken heart which we offer to You knowing that, לֵב נִשְׁבָּר וְנִדְכֶּה אֱלֹהִים לֹא תִבְזֶה, *God will never disdain a heart that is broken and contrite* (Psalms 51:19).

אַמִּיץ כֹּחַ ... ~§
O Vigorously Strong ...

There is today's Yom Kippur and there is that of yesteryear. There is today's Yom Kippur with its emphasis on *teshuvah* and *viduy* — a Yom Kippur, we might say, which is celebrated most authentically in each individual's contrite heart, where public prayer does no more than provide an appropriate setting for what is essentially a lonely encounter with one's God.

And then there is the Yom Kippur of the past. There, focus was upon the *Kohen Gadol* in the *Bais HaMikdash*, the people-as-a-whole held center stage, and individual identity was absorbed into the amorphous anonymity of the community.[1]

And yet — that Yom Kippur does not lie wholly in the past. The high-point of our *Mussaf* service is surely the moment when, as part of the *selichos*, we recite the *avodah*, the detailed account of the sacrificial service which, on this day, the *Kohen Gadol* performed in the *Bais HaMikdash*. For a few fleeting moments time-barriers seem to slip away. We are among the, *Kohanim and the people standing in the Courtyard*. We too can hear the, *glorious, awesome Name, the Ineffable One, emanating from the Kohen Gadol's mouth in holiness and purity*. We join eternal Israel as we, *kneel and prostrate ourselves, give thanks, fall upon*

---

1. The extent to which the community, rather than the individual, was recipient of the atonement which was elicited on the Yom Kippur of the Temple era, can be illustrated by the fact that the *sa'ir hamishtale'ach* atoned for certain levels of transgression even without the sinner's *teshuvah* (Rambam, *Hilchos Teshuvah* 1:2).

This can be understood only in the terms which we have suggested. The *sa'ir hamishtale'ach* is a קָרְבַּן צִבּוּר, *a communal sacrifice* and its efficacy extends to the community as whole. The individual shares in this gift to the extent that he has not forfeited his standing in the community. His individual *teshuvah* is not relevant.

our faces and say, "Blessed is the Name of His glorious kingdom for all eternity."

For those few moments at least, we are not alone. We rub shoulders, as it were, with generations long since gone, with communities from whom we are separated by continents and centuries. We lose ourselves — and find ourselves — in *Klal Yisrael*.

What does the recitation of the *avodah* say to us? What do we say to ourselves as we try to relive yesterday's glory?

❦ ❦ ❦

Our form of the *avodah* service, the initial words of which form the heading for this essay, is only one among many which were composed for this all-important segment of the *Mussaf selichos*. Thus, for example, there are two other, quite different, versions to be found in the *Siddur R' Saadya Gaon*. Many of these *avodahs* begin with a short survey of how God created the world, move on swiftly through history until they come to the choice of Levi as the tribe from which the *Kohanim* would descend, and only then take up their main theme.

Why this tendency? Why the sense that the *avodah* ought to be placed in the context of world history?

This convention is not limited to the *avodah*; it is reflected, too, in the *ne'ilah* service: *You set man apart from the beginning and You considered him worthy to stand before you, for who can tell You what to do ... Now You gave us, HASHEM our God with love, this Day of Atonement ...*

Clearly, once more, Yom Kippur as a *Day of Atonement* is not seen in isolation — as simply an annual chance to cleanse oneself of a destructive past and to renew and refresh one's commitment to serious living. Rather it is a logical and necessary outgrowth of God's inscrutable will to create man and to *set him apart* for a specific and significant destiny.

... For who can tell You what to do! The plaintive mystification is only too clear. We know ourselves so well. We know our rebellions and our carelessness, our lust and our pride.

Above all we know our vulnerability: our pathetic need to count, to be recognized; our propensity to purchase momentary and tarnished glory by putting down another. We know our lack of love, our greed, our sour ambitions which so easily disregard rights and sensibilities. We know, oh how we know, the sheer insignificance of many of our endeavors, the childishness of our needs, the cruelty of which we are capable, the ugly nastiness with which we lash out at those whom we perceive as threats to our self-respect.

Why, indeed, would God want us?

> When God wanted to create the first man, He sought counsel from the angels ...
>
> They said to Him, "This man, what is to be his nature?"
>
> He said to them, "Righteous people will descend from him."
>
> ... He informed them that righteous men will descend from him but did not tell them that wicked men, too, would descend from him. For, had he told this to them then the מִדַּת הַדִּין the *quality of justice*, would not have permitted him to be created. (*Bereishis Rabba* on נַעֲשֶׂה אָדָם).

Earlier in the *midrash* we are taught that in order to make the creation of man possible, God had to call upon the מִדַּת הָרַחֲמִים the *quality of mercy* — apparently to temper the objections of the מִדַּת הַדִּין.

This can only mean that man's existence flies in the face of logic. The מִדַּת הַדִּין, that quality which knows only balance and truth, which bases its decisions on nothing but the absolute rights and wrongs of a given situation, can find no justification for the injection of such imperfection into God's perfect world. רַחֲמִים is needed. That quality which knows dimensions beyond the strictly rational, where right is tinged with love, where balance is weighted in favor of the imperfect and the vulnerable, had to be harnessed in the service of the fulfillment of God's will.

What was that will? What stimulated it?
We quote *Bamidbar Rabba* 10:1.

> ...שׁוֹקָיו עַמּוּדֵי שֵׁשׁ (*Shir HaShirim* 5:15) [*His thighs are pillars of marble*. The passage describes the suitor who, in the poetic imagery of *Shir HaShirim* is, of course, God. Therefore, rather than take the word literally, the *midrash* offers the following explanation] שׁוֹקָיו refers to this world. God *longed* to create it. [שׁוֹק is derived from the root שקק, *to crave*.] This, in accordance with that which is written, וְעָלַי תְּשׁוּקָתוֹ, *His craving is focused upon me* (*Shir HaShirim* 7:11).
>
> Now how do we know that [indeed God has a *longing* for this world to exist]?
>
> For it is written, וַיְכֻלּוּ הַשָּׁמַיִם וְהָאָרֶץ (*Genesis* 2:1). Now the word וַיְכֻלּוּ implies a *craving* [תַּאֲוָה], as it is written, ...נִכְסְפָה וְגַם כָּלְתָה נַפְשִׁי, *My soul longed and even craved*... (*Psalms* 84:3).

Needless to say that expressions such as *longing* and *craving* as they relate to God are meant only לְשַׁבֵּר אֶת הָאֹזֶן, to permit the ear to pick up a familiar term, one which can lend some manageable meaning to concepts which would otherwise remain beyond us. But, what exactly is our ear supposed to hear? What does God's longing mean to us?

There is no doubt at all that, at this point, we must once more recall the passage from *Derech Hashem* ch.8 which we quoted in, *Who is like You Merciful Father ...*: God, above all, beyond all, and before all is a God of love. Love drove Him, as it were, to long for man — and to create a world to accommodate him, love and only love determines the extent to which justice — always subordinate to love — is to be invoked in the management of the human society which came about as a result.

And love demands that the impossible become commonplace, that time itself, that inexorable forward-flow, shall be reversed, and that today's *teshuvah* have the capability of turning yesterday's sin to merit (*Yoma* 26b).

For, let there be no mistake, *teshuvah* is incompatible with those laws of nature which creation called into being. Sin spells death [... *See I place before you life, coupled with good, and death, coupled with evil* (*Deuteronomy* 30:15), and death — when normalcy prevails —cannot be revoked. *Teshuvah*, so the Sages teach us, antedated the world [See *Pachad Yitzchak*, *Yom HaKippurim* 23:4]. It could not have been otherwise. *Teshuvah* makes no sense. It had, as it were, to be forced upon an unwilling world.

We have a paradox. God longs for man [וְעָלַי תְּשׁוּקָתוֹ, see above from *Bamidbar Rabbah*]. Man needs a predictable world within which to function — and that means iron-clad laws of nature. But he needs even more, the means to create a second chance for himself, an opportunity to remake a past, to recover from even lethal mistakes. And so, he needs *teshuvah*. And *teshuvah* is an anomaly, a defiant maverik in an otherwise orderly universe.

And God in defiance of His own laws *set man apart* ... — and gave him Yom Kippur.

※ ※ ※

Just as *teshuvah* functions in a world of its own, is governed by laws which share nothing at all with those we know from other contexts, so too Yom Kippur is, as it were, a swath cut out of time, responsive only to its own rhythms. It is the supernal masquerading in the guise of the temporal, eternity stuffed into twenty-four hours. Its mode is that of the *Kodesh HaKodoshim* in which space, that most essential of physical properties, has lost all meaning [see, *And Accompanied by a Shofar Blast Did You Appear to Them* ...].

On Yom Kippur the *Kohen Gadol* stands at the center of events. His is a life that is lived outside the confines of the ordinary. It is to be played out within the Temple walls (*Rambam*, *Klei Hamikdash* 5:7). The most basic human need — the craving to accompany a loved one on his last journey — is forbidden him (*Rambam, Klei Hamikdash* 5:5). As he enters the *Kodesh HaKodoshim* he, as it were, sheds his physicality. [Thus *Maharal's* explanation of why אֲבַק לָשׁוֹן הָרַע can find atonement only on Yom Kippur. See, *And Accompanied By a Shofar Blast Did You Appear To Them*.]

At the very high-point of the Yom Kippur service the miraculous impinges upon the mundane. The red strip which was tied atop the Temple entrance turns white as a sign that Israel was once more pure, its sins forgiven.

Yom Kippur, in short, is a day like no other. God stretches out His hand and plucks a moment out of infinite — and created — time, to defy His own laws of nature. Yom Kippurim is truly a *Yom Ke-Purim*, a kind of Purim when appearances deceive and the extraordinary truth about what appears to be so ordinary lies beneath the surface.

Teshuvah and Yom Kippur. These two are, for us, the great emancipators. They constitute the truth beneath the truth. They are the pillars which guarantee the world-order — and the rebels who defy it. God gave us Yom Kippur *because* He created man, and *in spite* of the fact that he created a natural environment in which, alone, he can function.

Truly,

... *Who can tell You what to do!*

❦ ❦ ❦

... כָּל אֵלֶה, *All this occurred when the Temple was on its foundation ...and the Kohen Gadol stood and ministered — his generation watched and rejoiced* ....

... אַשְׁרֵי עַיִן רָאֲתָה כָּל אֵלֶה, *Fortunate is the eye that saw all these; for the ear to hear it distresses our soul* ....

... אֲבָל עֲוֹנוֹת אֲבוֹתֵינוּ הֶחֱרִיבוּ נָוֶה, *But our forefather's iniquities destroyed the Temple* ....

... וּמֵרֹב עֲוֹנֵינוּ, *And because of our abundant iniquities we have — neither elevation-offerings nor sin-offerings* ....

And the *selichos* go on and on describing the terrible losses which we have sustained — the utter desolation of our *galus* situation in which only a faint memory of the former glory remains.

At the beginning of this essay we noted that, as we prostrate ourselves during the *avodah* service, it seems as though we were trying to project something of the past into the present. We attempt to experience — if only through such a tiny gesture — some of what our fathers must have felt in those heady moments, fraught, as they surely were, with terror and love, total self-abnegation mixed with proud and confident assurance that a better future lay within their grasp.

We asked: What does the recitation of the *avodah* say to us? What do we say to ourselves as we try to relive yesterday's glory?

Let us answer this question by asking another. Is it really true? Is today, when contrasted with yesteryear, really so pallid and depressing?

The answer is both yes and no. Of course, as the *piyutim* which we quoted above make clear, there is much that we do not have; much for which we must mourn.

But there is another side to that coin. It is true that Yom Kippur has moved from the community to the individual, from the Temple to the heart. But the Jewish individual is an עוֹלָם מָלֵא, an *entire world* (*Sanhedrin* 4:5), and the Jewish heart has room for a sanctuary within it [. . . בְּלִבָבִי מִשְׁכָּן אֶבְנֶה]. For all our smallness we can accomplish great things. And our *teshuvah* elicits precisely the same degree of atonement as did the שָׂעִיר הַמִּשְׁתַּלֵּחַ.

And so, perhaps, as we recite the *avodah* service, we are meant to look not only to our history but to our present. It is not to be only a memory of past intimacy but a celebration of the power which even now lies ready to our hands. After we have prostrated ourselves we can stand taller, and the tears which we shed for a splendor that is no more can, if we will but let them, nurture a knowledge that in our smallness we are yet great, and that the God Who often seems so distant is, in reality, as close as our longings and our love.

בָּרוּךְ שֵׁם כְּבוֹד מַלְכוּתוֹ לְעוֹלָם וָעֶד
Hail His Illustrious Kingship To All Eternity

One of the most moving moments in the Yom Kippur service comes, as we begin the weekday *maariv* immediately after *ne'ilah*. We have only now finished calling out the *sheimos*, among them, according to many *minhagim*, בָּרוּךְ שֵׁם כְּבוֹד מַלְכוּתוֹ לְעוֹלָם וָעֶד. The very walls shook as we proclaimed God's kingship.

But now, the weekday *maariv* has begun. As we do every night of the year we recite the שְׁמַע. As usual we follow the first verse with בָּרוּךְ שֵׁם כְּבוֹד מַלְכוּתוֹ לְעוֹלָם וָעֶד. And as we get there, we once more, as we do throughout the year, drop our voices to a whisper. A time lapse of only moments — a chasm in terms of what has happened to us. There is nothing else that, brings home with such force the reality of the end of the *Yamim Nora'im*. The ten days during which God was so close to us have passed — irretrievably —into history. We must, once more, come to grips with the ordinary. We can only hope that the Yom Kippur experience will have helped us to imbue that ordinariness with light and hope — that the ordinary will turn out to be not ordinary at all.

❊ ❊ ❊

The thundering בָּרוּךְ שֵׁם כְּבוֹד מַלְכוּתוֹ לְעוֹלָם וָעֶד of the *sheimos* is possible only today. The usual constraints are lifted. What at other times we dare only whisper, becomes a self-conscious principled roar of affirmation on Yom Kippur.

Why?

First, though: What precisely do the words, בָּרוּךְ שֵׁם כְּבוֹד מַלְכוּתוֹ לְעוֹלָם וָעֶד, mean?

For the moment we leave בָּרוּךְ aside. Its object is clearly the phrase, שֵׁם כְּבוֹד מַלְכוּתוֹ. How do we translate?

First, the word, שֵׁם.

In common with many other words, this one is extremely versatile and is used with many different connotations. Our tendency to translate it as *name* wherever it occurs crimps the wide range of subtle meanings which it can convey and often distorts our understanding of the many passages in which this rendering is simply inappropriate.

A good place from which to illustrate this point is *Deuteronomy* 28:58. There we hear of the dreadful punishments which we will have to suffer if we do not fear, ... אֶת הַשֵּׁם הַנִּכְבָּד וְהַנּוֹרָא הַזֶּה אֶת ה' אֱ-לֹהֶיךָ. Now, in this sentence, the words, אֶת ה' אֱ-לֹהֶיךָ are clearly in apposition to, הַשֵּׁם הַנִּכְבָּד. הַשֵּׁם, then, is identical in meaning with, ה' אֱ-לֹהֶיךָ. It is used to convey, not the concept of *name* as we understand it, but rather something of God Himself.[1]

Another example among many: *Job* 1:21 reads: ה' נָתַן וה' לָקַח יְהִי שֵׁם ה' מְבֹרָךְ. If it is Hashem Who gave, and Hashem Who took, it is clearly Hashem Himself, not His name in the conventional sense, Who is to be blessed

There are literally hundreds of cases in T'NaCh where שֵׁם carries the connotation which we have suggested. Take the first verse in אַשְׁרֵי. The second phrase in, אֲרוֹמִמְךָ אֱלוֹהַי הַמֶּלֶךְ וַאֲבָרְכָה שִׁמְךָ לְעוֹלָם וָעֶד, parallels the first. We are to bless Hashem, not the name by which He is called.

---

1. *Ibn Ezra* in his *Sefer HaShem* offers an etymological explanation of the word שֵׁם. It is related to the adverb שָׁם, *there*, the word that indicates location. A name *locates* its bearer in the sense that it serves as a substitute for the person. When we say that Reuven is wise, we mean not the letters of the name but the person who goes by that name. We are saying that the *man* who carries the name Reuven, is wise. The שֵׁם brings Reuven שָׁם, *there*.

Thus שֵׁם used for the Divinity might best be rendered *Presence*. We will find that in some of its compound uses, there is simply no English equivalent.

The usage is too clear to require any more examples, so we can now move to a verse which is closer in meaning to our phrase. In *Nehemiah* 9:5 we read: בָּרְכוּ אֶת ה' ... מִן הָעוֹלָם עַד הָעוֹלָם וִיבָרְכוּ שֵׁם כְּבֹדֶךָ. Once more it is clear that the שֵׁם כְּבֹדֶךָ of the second phrase parallels the 'ה of the first. In such a compound usage [comparable to שֵׁם תִּפְאַרְתֶּךָ in *II Chronicles* 29:13] we have no English equivalent for שֵׁם. The closest we can get would approximate a rendering like, ...*that in You which is illustrious*.

Now clearly, כְּבֹדֶךָ can readily be expanded into כְּבוֹד מַלְכוּתֶךָ [as in אַשְׁרֵי — where we have .. כְּבוֹד מַלְכוּתְךָ יֹאמֵרוּ], in which case our English translation would ignore שֵׁם, and render much as we have done in the title to this essay: *Your* or *His illustrious kingship*.

Now for the precise meaning of בָּרוּךְ. It seems strange that we would have to attempt a definition of this commonly used word in the present context, but it is necessary because the concept of a human being blessing God in the sense in which we normally take the word seems almost blasphemous. For the simplest rendering of the word we go to *Radak* in the *Sefer HaShorashim* who writes: Those instances in which we find מְבָרֵךְ as somethings humans do about God — we must understand the word as a synonym for *praise*, תְּהִלָּה.

Such uses of בָּרֵךְ are legion in our prayer book. Thus, for example in נִשְׁמַת: ... וּלְבָרֵךְ ... לְהוֹדוֹת לְהַלֵּל לְשַׁבֵּחַ לְפָאֵר, or in יִשְׁתַּבַּח: ... בְּרָכוֹת וְהוֹדָאוֹת ... שִׁיר וּשְׁבָחָה הַלֵּל וְזִמְרָה. The context makes the meaning eminently clear.

Hence our rendering of בָּרוּךְ as, *Hail!*

Why during the rest of the year, do we whisper these words, and why, on Yom Kippur can we say them loudly?

For the silent recitation during the rest of the year, *Tur* 61 cites *Pesachim* 56a:

> Jacob wished to reveal the *end* [קֵץ] to his children — but the Divine Spirit [שְׁכִינָה] left him. He said to himself, "Perhaps, God forbid, there are among my

children those that are unworthy, as Abraham had Ishmael and as Isaac had Easau?"

His sons said to him, שְׁמַע יִשְׂרָאֵל ה׳ אֱלֹ־הֵינוּ ה׳ אֶחָד. They said, "Just as in you heart there is only one so, too in our heart there is only one!. [In this context, יִשְׂרָאֵל refers to Jacob.]

When he heard this, Jacob said, בָּרוּךְ שֵׁם כְּבוֹד מַלְכוּתוֹ לְעוֹלָם וָעֶד.

Now the Sages said, "What shall we do [about our including בָּרוּךְ שֵׁם כְּבוֹד מַלְכוּתוֹ לְעוֹלָם וָעֶד in our recitation of the שְׁמַע?] Shall we say it? But our teacher Moses did not say it. Shall we not say it? But Jacob said it.

They decreed that it should be said silently.

... This is comparable to a princess who smelled a delicious dish [and craved it]. If she asks for it — it will embarrass her. If she does not ask for it — she will suffer pain. So her servants brought it to her in secret.

Our custom to recite בָּרוּךְ שֵׁם כְּבוֹד מַלְכוּתוֹ לְעוֹלָם וָעֶד silently is, then, grounded in the fact that it does not ap- pear in the Torah — our teacher Moses did not say it.

In *Hilchos Yom HaKipurim* 619 the *Tur* talks of the custom to say בָּרוּךְ שֵׁם כְּבוֹד מַלְכוּתוֹ לְעוֹלָם וָעֶד in a loud voice, on Yom Kippur. He traces it to a *midrash* which relates that when Moses went up to heaven to receive the Torah he heard these words of praise recited by the angels. He coveted their ability to laud God with these words and, so to speak, *stole* it from them. He brought the formula down and gave it to Israel.

What to do? We had it — but could lay no legitimate claim to it. How was this form of praise to be used?

Our predicament, so the *midrash* continues, can be compared to that of a man who stole a precious ornament from the palace and gave it to his wife. Certainly she could not flaunt it in public. He admonished her to wear it only in the house where nobody else would see it.

We, too, must treat these wonderful words gingerly. They are not really our's. It is only on Yom Kippur, when, denied all physical indulgences, we are like the angels to whom this praise is natural, that we permit ourselves to say it without shame.

The two sources, the one from *Pesachim* and the *midrashic* one appear to be unconnected.

We have a problem here. Not that two entirely different explanations are adduced for the same usage. As long as they do not contradict one another they can clearly coexist. There can be any number of equally potent reasons for anything we do. But how does our *minhag* on Yom Kippur square with the *Pesachim* passage. We may be like angels on Yom Kippur and therefore immune from the stricture of decking ourselves in stolen feathers, but what of the fact that, *Moses did not say it*? If this is enough reason to make us whisper the rest of the year, it ought to hold good on Yom Kippur too?

※ ※ ※

We will have to conclude that the two sources are, in fact, related. Moses did not say בָּרוּךְ שֵׁם כְּבוֹד מַלְכוּתוֹ לְעוֹלָם וָעֶד [*Pesachim*] *because* he had "stolen" it [midrash]. On Yom Kippur when the *midrashic* stricture is lifted — Moses too would have agreed with our father, Jacob, that it ought to be said.

What does all this mean?

Maharal, *Nesivos Olam*, in the seventh chapter of *Nesiv HoAvodah* tackles some of these problems. The solutions appear to touch upon profound mysteries and his ideas are presented and discussed with the requisite depth in *Rav Hutner's Pachad Yitzchak* to Yom Kippur. Here we must deal with the issues at a much more superficial level. Nevertheless we can avail ourselves of some of the thoughts which *Maharal* expresses even though we will obviously not plumb their full depth.

The passage in *Pesachim* is self-contained — that is, that it does not base itself in any way upon the *midrashic* passage which *Tur*

ונעילה — *Ne'ilah*

cites in *Hilchos Yom HaKippurim*. Clearly, then we must be able to understand it in its own terms.

Why could Moses not have said that which Jacob had no difficulty in saying? How are things made better by whispering the words instead of proclaiming them loudly?

Moses said ... בָּרוּךְ שֵׁם כְּבוֹד מַלְכוּתוֹ לְעוֹלָם but not שְׁמַע יִשְׂרָאֵל וָעֶד. Jacob permitted himself to say even בָּרוּךְ שֵׁם כְּבוֹד מַלְכוּתוֹ לְעוֹלָם וָעֶד. How are we to understand this?

With our knowledge of the *midrash* we can make the question more pointed: Jacob said בָּרוּךְ שֵׁם כְּבוֹד מַלְכוּתוֹ לְעוֹלָם וָעֶד, in a loud voice, without having been up to heaven. Apparently then, he had no need to "steal" these words from the angels, had no reason, therefore, to protect himself by saying them quietly. Why did Moses have to "steal" what Jacob possessed without any problems?

Based upon the *midrash*, it would appear that ... שְׁמַע יִשְׂרָאֵל and בָּרוּךְ שֵׁם כְּבוֹד מַלְכוּתוֹ לְעוֹלָם וָעֶד relate to one another. The latter seems to have been said in reaction to the former. What do they have in common? Above all, in the context of the problems which we are posing: In what way do they differ from one another? Why did Moses have no difficulty with ... שְׁמַע יִשְׂרָאֵל, and yet have to "steal" בָּרוּךְ שֵׁם כְּבוֹד מַלְכוּתוֹ לְעוֹלָם וָעֶד from the angels?

First, to an examination of what the two have in common. This will lead us to refine more precisely the meaning of בָּרוּךְ שֵׁם כְּבוֹד מַלְכוּתוֹ לְעוֹלָם וָעֶד. Where above we sought only to translate the words correctly, we must now seek the full range of their power.

First, שֵׁם. Above we suggested that this word could best be rendered as *Presence*. Based on *Michtav MeiEliyahu* Vol. 2 p.17, we take our analysis a stage further. From the usage of R' Meir, reported in *Yoma* 83b, to read profound insights into people's character through a careful investigation into their names [ר' מֵאִיר דָּיֵיק בִּשְׁמָא], *Rav Dessler* concludes that a name is that which reveals the true essence of him who bears it. We might understand this on the basis of *Amudei Shamayim* [quoted in *Kuntros Kri'as HaShem* in *R' Moshe Bunim Pirutinsky's Sefer HaBris*] who cites *Arizal* that: . . . No name is ever given by coincidence but [on the contrary] it all happens as a result of Divine intervention. Since it is clear [to God] what the essential nature and the activities of this person will be, the father is inspired to name him in accordance with this. For the name explicitly relates to the essence and activities of this man, whether in the direction of good or the direction of bad . . .

שֵׁם, then, denotes not only Presence, but also — Essence. When we talk of someone's שֵׁם, we are penetrating to the very deepest depths of his being.

Now כָּבוֹד: Normally translated as *honor* or, *respect*, this word derives from the root כבד, *to be heavy*. The thought transference from *weight* to *honor* is eminently reasonable when we consider that קָלוֹן, *disrespect* or *disparagement*, derives from קלל, *to be light*.

Thus, by means of its לָשׁוֹן הַקֹּדֶשׁ the Torah conveys to us the thought that respect and contempt are measured as forms of impact upon an outside observer. Just like weight has no meaning at all until someone outside the object attempts to grapple with it, so too, respect is, as it were, in the eyes of the beholder.

But, for the beholder to truly come to grips with the weight of the object, he needs to deal with it in its entirety. If he relies upon visual perception alone he may be greatly deceived. A huge balloon weighs much less than a compact piece of iron. The entire object must be known if its weight is to be determined. The entire person must be known if a correct assessment is to be made of whether he is deserving of respect or of disdain.

Thus, when we talk of כָּבוֹד, we are dealing with outer contours as they are augmented by inner realities. When we talk of כְּבוֹד מַלְכוּת, we must mean a true perception of its essence and nature.

אַחְדוּת, the concept of God's *oneness*, and מַלְכוּת, the idea of His Kingship, are congruent terms. Witness the fact that in proclaiming God as *one* [... ה׳ אֶחָד] we are accepting upon ourselves the yoke of his kingship — קַבָּלַת עוֹל מַלְכוּת שָׁמַיִם. Accordingly we can say that when we proclaim that the שֵׁם כְּבוֹד מַלְכוּתוֹ is to be lauded, we are really talking about His oneness, the same concept that is embedded in ... שְׁמַע יִשְׂרָאֵל.

We have now reached a point at which we realize that שְׁמַע יִשְׂרָאֵל ... and בָּרוּךְ שֵׁם כְּבוֹד מַלְכוּתוֹ לְעוֹלָם וָעֶד express essentially the same thought.

What, then, differentiates between them?

It is the fact that ... שְׁמַע יִשְׂרָאֵל is exhortative while בָּרוּךְ שֵׁם כְּבוֹד מַלְכוּתוֹ לְעוֹלָם וָעֶד expresses the innermost feelings of the person who pronounces it. The שְׁמַע is addressed to יִשְׂרָאֵל. It speaks to others. It seeks to encompass a whole nation in the enormity of its revelation. Listen Israel to what I have to say to you: God is One!

It cannot go beyond the audience to which its message is addressed. It is an ideal towards which all can strive, but in its fullest realization it lies in an eternal beyond which can challenge and goad — but which can never be fully attained.

Moses could, so to speak, address it to Israel without knowing for certain that it reflected the true state of belief of even one of them.

בָּרוּךְ שֵׁם כְּבוֹד מַלְכוּתוֹ לְעוֹלָם וָעֶד is different. It expresses the same idea, but as the absolute reflection of the speaker's beliefs.

It is the credo of the angels.

Small wonder that it excited Moses's envy. Would that it would have been possible to express each Jew's standing in such unambiguous terms.

But that could not be. People are not angels and their Torah cannot project a utopia. Moses could not write more than שְׁמַע יִשְׂרָאֵל ... — and hope that each individual would strive to make it true for himself.

And so he "stole" בָּרוּךְ שֵׁם כְּבוֹד מַלְכוּתוֹ לְעוֹלָם וָעֶד from the angels and bid us say it in a whisper.

What does that mean?

It means that there is something of the angel in man — immutable and firm, impervious to the erratic ups and downs which constitute the surface roilings of our tempestuous battles with temptation and pettiness. It means that there is a soul which — in spite of all that we do and leave undone, in spite of all that we make, or fail to make, of ourselves — remains pure and good.

That soul speaks in a whisper — its voice drowned in the turbulence of our constant battle with ourselves.

There are those whose sanctity is such that that inner voice can speak with confidence and authority. Jacob, the paradigmatic man of holiness [וְהִקְדִּישׁוּ אֶת קְדוֹשׁ יַעֲקֹב] could proclaim בָּרוּךְ שֵׁם כְּבוֹד מַלְכוּתוֹ לְעוֹלָם וָעֶד loud and clear for all the world to hear.

But for the rest of us that possibility does not exist.

Except on Yom Kippur.

Yom Kippur is the day on which, if we will but let it, our soul — our better self, that part of us of which we need not feel ashamed — comes into its own. We desist from eating, from drinking, from washing, from wearing shoes, from intimacy with our wives; in short from all those activities which, in the normal course of events are the source of our weaknesses and often, of our failings.

And so, on Yom Kippur the "Jacob" within each of us calls out, with passion and conviction, that which the rest of the year we dare no more than whisper. We count ourselves among those who have found within themselves the courage and conviction to proclaim that בָּרוּךְ שֵׁם כְּבוֹד מַלְכוּתוֹ לְעוֹלָם וָעֶד.

מָה אָנוּ מֶה חַיֵּינוּ... ❊
What Is Our Value?
What Is the Value of Our Lives?

There is nothing quite like it. The spine-chilling moment when, as that last emotion-charged hour of Yom Kippur is upon us, the אַשְׁרֵי of the *ne'ilah* service crashes upon our senses. There is love and there is terror. The familiar phrases of אַשְׁרֵי, worn smooth and glib throughout the year by countless repetition, are, for one precious moment, metamorphosed into pregnant, tear-choked affirmations of — we know not precisely what, know only that it is not what we always thought it was; know that it is infinitely deeper, infinitely more precious. There is the desperate awareness of opportunity slipping fast, too fast, into oblivion; the exquisite tension which dares to hope — but knows that hopes can so easily sputter out in sour frustration. There is the awareness of an utter worthlessness — which we know as capable of creating the fertile soil in which seeds of worth are bodied forth. There is the bent back; there is the soaring spirit. There is hunger and there are sore feet — and they matter not at all. It is the one moment in our Jewish lives in which we know beyond nagging doubt, beyond cowardly cavilling, that we can touch greatness. That it is wonderful to be a Jew.

And so, we are surprised. We have, throughout the day, become used to the probing, the ruthless penetration into the smallest and most private recesses of our being, which lie at the essence of the wondrous catharthis which the constant *viduyim* have provided. We are, as it were, longing for one more chance, one last opportunity to gaze into our past to discover and to excise. We look to the long and detailed litany of the עַל חֵטְא to lend form and structure to our scrutiny.

And we do not find it. There is an almost perfunctory bow, through the ... אָשַׁמְנוּ, to the obligation to be *misvadeh*, and then — nothing. There seems to be an almost conscious effort to, at this late hour, turn us towards a different direction. The *vidu'im* of the past have played their role. The צֹו הַשָּׁעָה, the *need of the moment*, is something different.

What? And, why?

❦ ❦ ❦

We need to know a little more about the meaning of *viduy* — although we have already discussed it at length in, *For We Are Not Brazen Faced* ..., and we need to analyze in depth the nature of the *ne'ilah* service.

First, *viduy*.

> What is he to say [for *viduy*]? Said Rav, *You know the secrets of the universe* .... R' Yochanan said, *Master of the universe. [It is not with reliance upon our righteousness that we pour out our entreaties before You (Rashi)]*. ... Rav Hamnuna said, *My God, before I was formed I was unworthy, and now that I have been formed, it is as though I was not formed. I am dust in my life and will surely be so in my death. Behold — before You I am like a vessel filled with shame and humiliation. May it be Your will ... that I not sin again. And what I have sinned before You, may You cleanse with Your abundant mercy ....*
>
> Mar Zutra said: "All this applies only if he has not said, אֲבָל אֲנַחְנוּ חָטָאנוּ. But if he said, אֲבָל אֲנַחְנוּ חָטָאנוּ, there is no need to say anything else." (*Yoma* 87b)

Whether or not Mar Zutra's, אֲבָל אֲנַחְנוּ חָטָאנוּ is meant to stand on its own or whether he means it as the introductory phrase to the ... אָשַׁמְנוּ litany, is, for us, a moot question. It is, however, quite clear from his words, that the other *amora'im* did not say that or any similar formula. Their *viduy* consisted solely of the passages which the Gemara records.

But, in what sense can these musings and prayers be regarded as *viduy*? Certainly they contain no hint of confession?

We quote our thoughts from the previous essay concerning the underlying dynamics of *viduy* as it is expressed in the *hispa'el* form of the root, ידה.

> Certainly מוֹדֶה, in the *kal* could serve to describe the act of confession as readily as it can take on the meaning, to praise or to thank. But, it would not, in that voice, do justice to the full implication of what the act of *viduy* before God requires. *Viduy* is to be much more than a simple admission. It must entail a gut-wrenching inner dislocation, a ruthless probing that plays havoc with the veneer of big and little frauds which, in ordinary circumstances, we use so efficiently to allay our conscience. It must lay bare the innermost recesses of our being to the harsh and unforgiving light of truth, it must leave us shattered and broken by the sheer enormity of the lie we have been living.
>
> We do not simply *cast ourselves down* before God [מוֹדֶה]. We undergo a metamorphosis. We become nothing more than deflated relics of our wicked bombast. We have nothing left but our — *prostration*. We define ourselves by only its terms, know no truth besides our fall. There is nothing left to us but that we are a mass of collapsed potentialities, the sorry remnants of high hopes gone sour [מִתְוַדֶּה].

Confession, then, in the sense of admitting to sins committed, is only one form that *viduy* might take. Certainly a confrontation with one's own sheer wickedness is an effective way of generating the sense of dislocation of which we spoke. But — it is not the only way. Need not indeed, in some situations, be necessarily the best way. The *amora'im* whom the Gemara quotes, apparently felt that, for themselves at least, their own idiosyncratic ruminations might be more effective [But see *Sefas Emes* to *Yoma* 87b who suggests that the wordings used by the various *amora'im* were only introductions [דברי פתיחה] to the actual *viduy*].[1]

---

1. In our quotation of the *Yoma* passage we did not list all the different *viduyim* which the Gemara ascribes to various *amora'im*. We cited only those which have, since then, found a place in our own *tefillah*. Rav's is the passage which begins with the words, ... אַתָּה יוֹדֵעַ רָזֵי עוֹלָם — a regular feature of all of our Yom Kippur *viduyim*, as is also R' Hamnuna's, ... אֱ‍לֹ-הַי עַד שֶׁלֹּא נוֹצַרְתִּי. R' Yochanan's prayer, ... רִבּוֹן כָּל הָעוֹלָמִים, appears in our every-day *Shacharis* service, and sections of it, ... מָה אָנוּ, have been incorporated in the *Ne'ilah*.

This is worthy of note. The very fact that the Gemara records how each of the *amora'im* had said his own, personal *viduy*, indicates that *viduy* is, as we would expect it to be, very much an individual matter, and the thoughts which are effective for one person might well not touch another. Why, then institutionalize the words of this or that *amora* thus making it a part of every person's *viduy*? Does such standardization not rob the words of their soul?

We have an analogous situation in *Berachos* 16b and 17a. There the Gemara records the devotions with which various *amora'im* used to conclude their silent *amidah* prayers. The mere fact that the Gemara possessed records of so many individual prayers demonstrates that there was no attempt at all at standardization and that, on the contrary, the sense of our sages was that the silent devotions with which we are to end the *amidah* are to be an opportunity for each of us to personalize our prayers.

Nevertheless, it has become customary for us to conclude our *amidah* with, ... אֱ‍לֹ-הַי נְצוֹר לְשׁוֹנִי מֵרָע, which was the ending used by Mar Brei de'Ravina, but by none of the other *amora'im*.

Once more we have a thrust at standardization which seems to fly in the face of the need for spontaneity which appears to have prompted the original usage.

One must suppose that these customs developed in response to a general feeling of inadequacy — a fear that we lack the fluency of language and the sense of what is and what is not appropriate which should certainly precede any attempt at formulating our own prayers.

Nevertheless, the knowledge that ideally these devotions should be personalized ought to spur us to struggle for some degree of originality. See *Mishnah Berurah* 122:8.

We conclude that *viduy* need not necessarily take the form of confession.

Now, for a closer look at the *Ne'ilah* service.

We quote *Yoma* 87b:

> ... There are three occasions upon which the *kohanim* recite the Priestly Blessing four times during the day — at *Shacharis*, *Mussaf*, *Minchah* and *ne'ilas she'arim* [the Closing of the Gates].
>
> ... What is *ne'ilas she'arim*? Rav said: It is a prayer which is added on [above and beyond the usual number of daily prayers]. (It consists of seven *berachos* as do the other daily prayers [*Rashi*]). Shmuel said: [It is not a regular *tefillah* (*Rashi*) but simply the recitation of מָה אָנוּ מֶה חַיֵּינוּ].[2]

Before we try to understand the argument between Rav and Shmuel we should spend a few moments discussing the term, *ne'ilas she'arim*, the closing of the gates. Which *gates* are meant here?

We suspect that most of us, as we entreat God to, *Open the gate for us at this time when the gate closes* ..., [פְּתַח לָנוּ שַׁעַר בְּעֵת ... נְעִילַת שַׁעַר] have in our mind's eye those gates which began to open a crack as the first shofar blast of Elul ushered in the month of love, which swung wide as with the advent of Rosh Hashanah the עֲשֶׂרֶת יְמֵי תְּשׁוּבָה made God accessible to even the least worthy among us, and which finally, on Yom Kippur beckoned us onwards and upwards to the cleanliness and sanctity

---

2. *Meromey Sadeh* has a problem with Shmuel's opinion. If indeed *ne'ilah* consists solely of the recitation of ... מָה אָנוּ, that is, that it does not have the form and structure of a regular *tefillah* — then it cannot possibly be accompanied by the Priestly Blessing. בִּרְכַּת כֹּהֲנִים can only take place as a part of an עֲבוֹדָה which, outside the Temple, requires the formal structure of *tefillah*.

Because of this problem he postulates that even Shmuel would agree that the ... מָה אָנוּ passage must be followed by the blesing, ... רְצֵה, which is the עֲבוֹדָה blessing in our regular daily prayer.

of which this day of days whispers to us and to which it summons us — in short, the שַׁעֲרֵי תְשׁוּבָה.

But — this is not, indeed cannot be, the correct translation. We recall from the passage quoted above, that besides on Yom Kippur there were two other times when the *kohanim* recited the Priestly Blessing four times — that is, that a fourth service, that of *ne'ilas she'arim* was performed. The daily מַעֲמָדוֹת, *prayers offered up in conjunction with the Temple service*, comprised a fourth service called *ne'ilas she'arim*, as did the תַעֲנִיוֹת, the special *fast-days* which were instituted in times of drought or other national disasters.

Clearly, then, the *gates* are not any which are specifically associated with the environment of Yom Kippur.

What, then, are these closing *gates*?

Rav and Rabbi Yochanan argue in *Yerushalmi*, *Berachos* 4:1. Rav thinks that the *Gates of Heaven* are meant. The prayer is to be said at night when, as it were, the gates of heaven have closed over the sun and darkness has fallen. Rabbi Yochanan disagrees: Reference is to the Temple Gates. *Ne'ilah* is to be recited when these gates are closed for the night — that is, while there is still daylight.

Rambam (*Tefilah* 1:7) codifies Rav's opinion: The Sages also instituted another prayer to be recited after *Minchah* close to sunset. This is only to be said on fast days so that the fast might generate additional prayers and entreaties. This is the prayer which is known as *Ne'ilah*, that is to say: The *Gates of Heaven* have closed in over the sun which has now disappeared. This, because [*ne'ilah*] can only be said close to sunset.

Rambam's insistence that *Ne'ilah* be said close to sunset is readily understood. The very name of this service, *Ne'ilah*, the closing, implies this relationship. But, why should this be so? What inner connection can there be between this service and the setting sun [or, according to Rabbi Yochanan, the closing Temple gates]?

Moreover: What is so evocative about a setting sun or a closing Temple gate? Why, פְּתַח לָנוּ שַׁעַר בְּעֵת נְעִילַת שַׁעַר?

🦋 🦋 🦋

Our quest for understanding takes us to *Berachos* 29b. The Gemara's discussion centers upon the Mishnah which had taught that prayer must not be static or bland [קֶבַע]. What, the Gemara wonders, would be such an uninspired prayer?

> [A person could be described as making his prayer קֶבַע if] he does not pray with the changing sun [עִם דִמְדוּמֵי חַמָּה]. [That is, the morning *amidah* at the moment of sunrise, the *Minchah amidah* at the moment of sunset.]
>
> ... [Nevertheless] In the west [the Land of Israel] they would frown upon anyone who would pray [*Minchah*] at sunset. This, because by waiting until the last possible moment he exposes himself to the possibility of missing the correct time for the *Minchah* prayer altogether.

Rashi explains that the moment of sunrise and sunset is one of particular good will on the part of God [עֵת רָצוֹן]. The person who makes no special effort to pray at such a propitious time is clearly interested only in fulfilling the minimum that he is called upon to do. His heart is not in his prayer.

What is so special about this particular moment, and why, if it is so special, were the people of the west so set against the practice?

The moments of sunrise and sunset evoke deep feelings within us. All the hope, the confidence, the young and fresh vigor of the morning — the mood that should inform our *Shacharis* — is vested in the moment that the sun rises majestically above the horizon. In the evening, the setting sun, the approaching darkness with its dreads and threatening portent sets the tone for the somber *Minchah* service.

When we choose those moments to stand in prayer before God, we are, as it were, fusing our whispers into the symphony of worship which nature in all its variegated tones and moods offers up to God. Our hearts resonate to universal adoration, we are wafted upwards and inwards — and God accepts our prayers with good will [עֵת רָצוֹן] as He finds satisfaction in the wondrous creation which, in myriad voices forged into one harmony, so declares His glory.

In such a *tefillah* there is no קֶבַע. No stale mechanization, no deadened mind, no mouthing of words denuded of meaning by numbing rote.

And yet — the people of the west would have none of it. The most exquisite of feelings, the most profound emotions, must yield to the *halachah*. There is nothing, literally nothing, which is as important as living as God would have us live. And that Divine will is reflected in the *halachah*. The most fervent prayer, if it is uttered after the time assigned to it, is — in terms of fulfilled obligations — meaningless. For *Minchah* we cannot risk waiting for the setting sun. Better a less inspired prayer — but one which hews to the *halachic* norm (*Siddur Olas Re'iyah*).

Ne'ilah appears to be different. The *Rambam* whom we quoted above, writes explicitly that it is to be recited *after Minchah, close to sunset*. At the end of the passage he repeats himself, lending the point particular significance. *Ne'ilah* can *only* be said close to sunset. No hesitation, no fearfulness here lest by waiting to the last moment the time may pass altogether. Our entreaty, בְּעֵת נְעִילַת פְּתַח לָנוּ שַׁעַר is to be made specifically and exclusively, שַׁעַר.[3]

---

3. For an analysis of what precisely *Rambam* means by שְׁקִיעָה which we have rendered *sunset*, see *Magen Avraham* and *Taz* to *Orech Chaim* 623:1. Whether we assume with *Taz* that the "beginning" of שְׁקִיעָה is meant, that is the actual sunset, or with *Magen Avraham* that the "end" of שְׁקִיעָה, the equivalent of צֵאת הַכּוֹכָבִים is the cut-off point, it is clear from *Rambam* that there *is* some point beyond which *Ne'ilah* cannot be recited. This is the basis for the argument which we make within.

There are times when boldness must be the order of the day. We need the setting sun, need that our hearts resonate to a gathering darkness which speaks to us with urgency of light's sweet allure. We need that our knowledge of precious time slipping into oblivion be reinforced by the sun dipping, too fast and beyond recall, below the threatening horizon. Not only our minds, but our senses must be engaged. It is *Ne'ilah*! The time of the closing of the gates!

❊ ❊ ❊

What is the *machlokes* between Rav and Shmuel? Better: What is Shmuel's thinking? Is not Rav's concept of a צְלוֹתָא יְתֵירָה, an extra *amidah*, the more logical? Shmuel's idea of a simple passage, . . . מָה אָנוּ seems artificial. It has no parallel, the more so if we accept *Meromey Sadeh's* suggestion that the passage is to be followed by . . . רְצֵה. Does not the fact that the ברייתא lists *Ne'ilah* in the same context with, *Shacharis*, *Mussaf* and *Minchah* seem to indicate that it is of a piece with them? Why does Shmuel go out of his way, as it were, to avoid the simple, the easy to understand?

We suspect that what we have learned above can go a long way towards explaining Shmuel. Moreover we shall see that even Rav is not so distant from Shmuel's thinking.

Ne'ilah, the moment of the setting sun, is the moment of perfect self-abnegation. It is a moment — so Shmuel feels — in which we want only one overwhelming thought to occupy our minds: . . . מָה אָנוּ מֶה חַיֵּינוּ. Even the formality of a *tefillah* is too much. With *Avos*, with *Gevuros*, with *Kedushah* and finally with *Kedushas HaYom* other thoughts, other emotions impinge upon us. But — significant as these are — now is not the time for them. The less we say the greater the intensity with which it takes hold of us, the more glaring and overpowering the dreadful מָה.

Rav, to some extent, appears to agree. Not only because he incorporates Shmuel's . . . מָה אָנוּ passage into his צְלוֹתָא יְתֵירָה

—assuming that the wording which we use goes back to his time — but because he, too, seems intent upon shortening and uncomplicating what we say.

We began our essay by asking why the ... עַל חֵטְא litany is missing from our *Ne'ilah* service. It seems almost certain that it is omitted in order to narrow the gap between Rav and Shmuel. If Shmuel elects to leave out the entire *tefillah* structure, we too will build our prayer in such a way that intensity will preponderate over volume.

The Shofar and the Nail

After [the *Ne'ilah* prayer is over] we blow the shofar [in recognition of the departure of the Divine Presence (סִימָן לְסִלּוּק שְׁכִינָה)] (*Taz* to *Orech Chaim* 623:6)]

... Those who take the *mitzvos* seriously [הַמְדַקְדְּקִים] begin the building of the succah immediately on the night of Yom Kippur (*Ramo* to *Orech Chaim* 625:5).

... One Yom Kippur night, after he returned from the synagogue, the Vilna Gaon said to R' David Shmuel Feigash of Vilna: "It is customary to fix a nail in the succah immediately after Yom Kippur. Come let us do just that." He took him into a room, took down a Gemara Succah, and studied with him the entire night. The Gaon said to him: "See, this is the "nail" which I have fixed firmly in place [יָתֵד בְּמָקוֹם נֶאֱמָן].(*Eidus Ne'manah* in *Ru'ach Eli'ahu* by *Rabbi E. Bloch*).

If we would have ended our series of essays with the previous one, if the *Ne'ilah* would have brought our Yom Kippur to a close, we would have missed an extremely important dimension. Yom Kippur must not, and does not, end for us with the departure of the Divine Presence. The יָתֵד נֶאֱמָן, the nail firmly hammered into the succah wall defies the shofar. We have our own means, so to speak, to hold on to the שְׁכִינָה.[1]

---

1. We do not want to place too heavy an emphasis on the Gaon's statement that it is customary to *fix a nail* into the succah immediately after Yom Kippur. I have not been able to find this particular formulation in any of the sources. *Ramo* to *Orech Chaim* 624:4 and 625:1 notes only that the succah ought to be started, and subsequently completed as close to Yom Kippur as possible. His language is more or less reflected in the other *poskim* and, to

Why the rush to begin the building of the succah immediately after Yom Kippur? Why, for that matter, does the *Yom Tov* of Succos come in such close proximity to Yom Kippur?

Surely there is a message here. We are to move straight from our Yom Kippur experience into the succah.

And what does that mean?

We should turn to *Sefas Emes* who again and again, by diverse routes and while stressing different facets of the same general theme, returns to the same central idea: The succah is God's protective embrace in which we need to lose ourselves and find shelter if we are to safeguard Yom Kippur's gift.

Yom Kippur's atoning function is *redemptive* — יוֹם יִשְׁעִי, זֶה יוֹם הַכִּפּוּרִים. It is redemptive in the sense that *Maharal* whom we quoted above in *The Entire Family of Israel Shall Be Forgiven*..., takes it:

> ... for Yom Kippur is a day of personal salvation. For when a person sins, the sin enslaves him and on Yom Kippur he goes free from this sin. And that is the thought behind the shofar blast on the night when Yom Kippur ends. For a shofar blast hints at going free as did the shofar of the Yom Kippur of the *Yovel*.

See in that essay for a wide-ranging discussion of this concept.

Now, freedom begets responsibility. Life, which in the past was a drudgery, circumscribed by another's whim, directed at

---

the best of my knowledge, no specific mention of *fixing a nail* is made by any of them.

Nevertheless the reference to the יָתֵד נֶאֱמָן, the *firmly embedded nail* (the source is from *Isaiah* 22:23 and 25) seems to indicate that these are in fact the words which the Gaon actually used. They may well reflect a custom that was prevalent in his time. People, in order to honor the *Ramo's* insistence that some start be made upon the building of the succah immediately after Yom Kippur, would, at the very least, do the minimum — that is, hammer in one nail.

The picture is, of course, an evocative one. Hammering in a nail conveys a sense of stability and permanence — ideas which are well in consonance with our thoughts in this essay.

another's behest, suddenly becomes something to be cherished and nurtured. It must be treasured and — protected. When the Egyptian shackles finally slipped off our arms we travelled from Raamses to סוכות — there to lose ourselves — and secure our new-found freedom — within the loving embrace of the עֲנְנֵי כָּבוֹד. In our *Ma'ariv* prayer we immediately follow the expression of gratitude for our redemption [גָּאַל יִשְׂרָאֵל ...] with a prayer that God spread His protective succah over us [וּפְרוֹשׂ עָלֵינוּ סוּכַּת שְׁלוֹמֶךָ].

And from Yom Kippur we hasten into the succah.

We do not trifle with the gift of purity and newly-minted innocence which this day of days has bestowed upon us. It is as yet too tender, too fragile to allow it to be buffeted by the careless and ruthless turbulence of daily living. The ordinary, the sheer comfortable familiarity of routine can be dangerously seductive. It seeks desperately to lull us into the somnolence from which we have only now escaped. It conspires to suck us back into the sour spiritual stagnation which so recently delimited the grim reality of our religious sterility. We dare not expose ourselves — yet — to the crushing, smothering mass of the every-day. We need to incubate the seed of sanctity which we now, so precariously, harbor within our souls.

And so — we make our way into the succah. It is, as it were, our way of extending the Yom Kippur experience. On Yom Kippur the *Shechinah* had been with us. But the shofar-blast at the end of the day had heralded its departure. We build the succah — and invite it back. The שֵׁם שָׁמַיִם rests upon the succah (*Succah* 9a). It is an anachronism, a small island of sanctity holding its own against the roaring breakers of the profane which are kept at bay by the modest walls which define the ambit of our temporary lives.[2]

---

2. It seems significant that the succah does not need to be walled in on all its four sides. Two walls and a piece of a third one are enough to satisfy the *halachah's* requirement.

How does the succah afford us protection?

It does so by placing the imprint of its sanctity upon every aspect of our living. Nothing is excluded from its embrace. Our eating and drinking, our sleeping, even the time we spend in undirected, religiously neutral activities [מְטַיֵּיל] — all are sublimated, all partake of the special flavor of *mitzvah*. For seven short days we live the life of which at other times we can only dream. How we would love it if we could always be good, if the grace of holiness could touch even our most mundane activities! And Succos tells us that it is possible. Succos tells us how a "Yom Kippur Jew" really looks.

But Succos does not portray the world as it really is. Its very structure tells us that it is a temporary — never a permanent — dwelling. It tantalizes us with an experience of the ideal — and then sends us out upon our way.

But it does not send us unequipped. We leave with a gift which it alone — not Rosh Hashanah and not Yom Kippur — has given us. It is the gift of love. On Rosh Hashanah and on Yom Kippur we learn to fear God. On Succos we learn to love Him. It could not be otherwise. As God gathers us — His very own — into His [עֲנָנֵי כָבוֹד], [. . . הֱבִיאַנִי אֶל בֵּית הַיָּיִן], we can respond only thus [כִּי .. חוֹלַת אַהֲבָה אָנִי].

※ ※ ※

Let us analyze this love a little more closely.

We have, up to this point, concentrated upon the succah. But — there is more to Succos than the succah. There are the אַרְבָּעָה

The symbolism, particularly that of the incomplete third wall is evocative. It seems to seek to reassure us. Do not be afraid of the secular world to which, inevitably, you will have to return. Two protective walls are sufficient — provided only that these two stretch out just a little more in a suggestive fencing off which, with good-will and determination can lend the character of separateness to all that is, so to speak, contained within the two complete walls. The very incompleteness of the succah walls bodes well for the time when we

Ne'ilah / נעילה

מִינִים, *the four species* which we wave before God as symbol of the inexpressible joy which we feel during this wonderful week. What do these have to say to us?[3]

There is a remarkable *midrash* which assigns the four species a function which we would not have divined from the simple meaning of the passage in *Emor*. They are symbols not only of a generous harvest which has filled our silos to bursting, but of a triumph only now wrested from a mighty battle from which we have emerged unscathed.

How so?

We already know Rosh Hashanah as a day of judgment upon which both individuals and the community must render an accounting. But, there is something more. On this day we are haunted, not only by a past for which we have only ourselves to blame, but by an enemy from without. The nations, like jackals smelling a kill, lurk hungrily in the background. In the moment of our perceived weakness they are ready to pounce with a claim which challenges our very life-blood as a people — our choseness. They demand equality before God.

And on Succos God confirms our uniqueness. The proud *lulav*, the comely *esrog*, the sweet-smelling *hadassim*, the stalwart, unexceptional *aravos* combine to proclaim our victory.

How?

Based upon various *midrashic* traditions recorded in *Yalkut Shimoni* to *Emor*, we may, perhaps, suggest as follows:

Rabbi Akiva taught: פְּרִי עֵץ הָדָר [the *esrog*] — that refers to God, as it is written [concerning Him], הוֹד וְהָדָר לָבָשְׁתָּ. כַּפֹּת תְּמָרִים [the *lulav*] — that refers to God, as it is written [concerning Him], צַדִּיק כַּתָּמָר יִפְרָח. וְעֲנַף עֵץ עָבוֹת [the *hadassim*] — that refers to God, as it is written [concerning Him], וְהוּא עוֹמֵד בֵּין הַהֲדַסִּים. וְעַרְבֵי

---

3. It is a fact that *poskim* suggest that it is a good idea not only to begin building the succah immediately after Yom Kippur, but also to use this time to make sure that the *esrog* which he intends to use meets the stringent requirements of הִדּוּר as it should. See *Matteh Ephraim* 624.

נָחַל [the *aravos*] — that refers to God, as it is written [concerning Him], סֹלּוּ לָרֹכֵב בָּעֲרָבוֹת.

The four species, then, all symbolize God.

Further, in the *midrash*, there:

פְּרִי עֵץ הָדָר [the *esrog*] — that is Israel. Just as the *esrog* has a fragrance and it can be eaten, so too there are people in Israel who both know the Torah [that which sustains and nurtures, analogous to food] and perform good deeds [spreading a delightful fragrance through their actions.] כַּפֹּת תְּמָרִים [the *lulav*] — that is Israel. Just like the fig sustains but has no fragrance, so too there are people in Israel who know the Torah but have no good deeds. כַּפֹּת תְּמָרִים [the *hadassim*] — that is Israel. Just as the myrtle has a fragrance but does not sustain, so too there are people in Israel who do good deeds but who have no Torah. וְעַרְבֵי נָחַל [the *aravos*] — that is Israel. Just as the *aravah* has neither fragrance nor food value, so there are people in Israel who have neither Torah nor good deeds.

The four species, then, symbolize Israel.

What, then, are we to conclude from the fact that they stand for both God and Israel?

There can be only one answer. When we wave the four species we are really celebrating a unison between God and Israel that is so close that it constitutes an actual fusing. The *esrog* is God and it is Israel. The *lulav* is God and it is Israel. The *hadassim* are God and they are Israel. The *aravos* are God and they are Israel. We rejoice before God because they are one.

And that oneness is the source of our choseness. The four species are the proud affirmation of the uniqueness which the nation's challenge on Rosh Hashanah could not shake.

They are the affirmation of undying love during Succos, the festival of love.

❧ ❧ ❧

And so, from Yom Kippur, we move to Succos and from Succos we move out into the humdrum and threatening world.

ונעילה — *Ne'ilah*

But there is a way station along our path. It is שְׁמִינִי עֲצֶרֶת, the most mysterious and undefined of all our *yamim tovim*.

How are we to understand this *yom tov* which, alone among our holy days has absolutely no *mitzvah* of its own [even Shavuos has its שְׁתֵּי הַלֶּחֶם] and which seems to exist in a kind of limbo — as part of Succos [*On the eighth day . . .*] and yet not as part of it [it's own שֶׁהֶחֱיָנוּ, and so on.]?

There is really only one possible explanation. *Shmini Atzeres* is Succos without the succah. It invites us back into our homes, and we find them — because we know ourselves to be — transformed. The solid ceiling above us is — we know it — no more than a facade, and our mind's eye can see the beckoning stars urging us onwards and upwards.

Shmini Atzeres is the final moment of intimacy which we share with God before we leave the *Yamim Nora'im* behind us. We have worked hard to achieve this day, have suffered hard and prayed — oh how we have prayed — that we might live it, really live it, in our hearts. For, without any *mitzvos* at all to shift the focus outwards, it is only in our hearts that we can and therefore must experience it.

❧ ❧ ❧

And so, the nail vanquishes the shofar. It, as it were, holds the departing *Shechinah* in its tracks and brings it again to dwell — more permanently if more hidden, among us.

With the passing of the last sacred moment of *Shmini Atzeres* we slip once more into the ordinary — the first moments of that eternity which began to be forged on Rosh Hashanah.